TO LOVE AGAIN

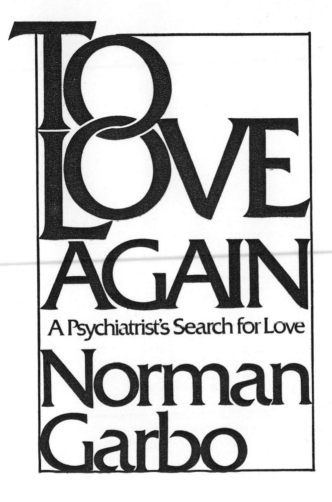

TO LOVE AGAIN

A Psychiatrist's Search for Love

Norman Garbo

McGraw-Hill Book Company

*New York   St. Louis   San Francisco   Düsseldorf
Mexico   Toronto*

Book design by Ingrid Beckman.

1234567890   FGFG   7832100987

Library of Congress Cataloging in Publication Data

Garbo, Norman.
To love again.
1. Psychotherapy—Philosophy.   2. Love. I. Title.
RC437.5.G37   616.8'9'00924 [B]   77-4171
ISBN 0-07-022815-9

All names used in this book are fictitious.

My gratitude to Arthur Pine, who has consistently proven himself to be the rarest and most luminous of living creatures, a literary agent with heart.

Preface

IT WAS A MODEST OBITUARY, only about three column-inches in the Sunday *Times*, and I almost missed it. As it was, the name Robert Flavin did not immediately register. Then I read about his having been a psychiatrist with a practice in Great Neck and New York and realized it was Bob. The obituary said he had died of cancer at Columbia Presbyterian, had been forty-two years old, and was survived by two children and a divorced wife. Other than a few additional details about his studies and work, that was pretty much all there was. And I thought, insanely—not a word about his backhand.

I don't suppose we had ever really been close

friends, at least not in the accepted sense. We had simply belonged to the same tennis club for about ten years and had enjoyed sitting around, talking over a drink after playing. We had never seen one another away from the courts, and inasmuch as the club was only open from May through September, seven months of each year we did not talk at all. With his death occurring in late April, virtually this entire period had elapsed since our last meeting. Time enough, obviously, to sicken and die; yet my last remaining memory of him was of a youthful, smiling, sun-browned man in tennis shorts.

Certainly that made it no easier to accept the idea of his being dead. On the court, he was fast and tireless, with an aggressive style of play and an incredible backhand. The only weakness in his game was an emotionalism that destroyed his consistency when he was under pressure. It was his business to understand such things and he did, but he was unable to help himself. I beat him every time. Each year he was sure this would be the year he would get even. He never did. When we said goodby in the fall, his last words were, "Wait till next year. Next year I'll really whip your ass."

He was intrigued by what I did for a living. I was in the arts, a painter and a writer. He liked to say he was also involved in one of the arts—psychiatry. He laughed at the idea of psychiatry as a science. "Of course we wrap ourselves in fine, scientific cloaks, but all we actually do is state unproven theories as facts, then try to mold our patients to fit the theories." He was that kind of irreverent, self-mocking guy. I found it refreshing in a member of a profession that tended to produce pompous oracles. In short, I liked the man.

I do not usually set much store in funerals and avoid them whenever possible, but I wanted to go to his. It embarrassed me: to have to admit the need of a final gesture of this sort was not easy for me. But I went. It was one of those modern, civilized funerals without wailing or breast-beating that go off with the precision and split-second timing of a well-planned military operation. His parents were dead, but I was able to pick out his ex-wife and teen-aged son and daughter from their proximity to the casket. The kids looked stiff and unhappy in their mourning clothes and the ex-wife appeared properly solemn, but I saw no tears on their faces. In fact I saw no tears anywhere, and it did not seem right. Somehow, at the end of his life, a man, any man, had the right to expect a few tears— at least from his children. Even if he had been a lousy father, which I doubt. Of course you never know what happens in a divorce—the best of couples seem to end up with the knives out and the blood running. Still, the man was their *father*, for God's sake!

Driving home from the cemetery, with the sky clear, the air warm, and the first azaleas beginning to blaze, I thought, What a goddamn backhand, and wept.

About two weeks later the carton arrived. It came by special delivery and carried the return address of a New York law firm. Inside was a pile of dated and consecutively numbered recording tapes, and a brief, handwritten note on the stationery of Robert Flavin, M.D.

Dear Norman,

Apparently I'm not going to whip your ass this year after all. By the time you read this note I'll probably be several weeks dead. I hope you have read or heard of this fact before now, so it doesn't come as a complete surprise. If it does, I'm sorry, but the enclosed tapes should explain the whole thing. Just be sure to listen to them in the proper sequence. The tapes are yours. Do anything you wish with the material in them. Or do nothing. Again, I apologize for the possible shock as well as the brevity of this note. I hate writing. Especially when I'm dead. A terrible joke, but as you know, I never could resist the worst of them.

BOB

There was also a letter from the law firm, identifying itself as the executor of the will of the late Robert Flavin and explaining that the enclosed material had been sent to me according to their client's instructions.

Characteristically, I did not own a tape player. Uncharacteristically, I went out and bought one. I suppose I might have borrowed a machine, but this somehow would not have seemed right. I spent the better parts of several days listening to the tapes. Then I let some time go by and listened to them twice more. They were all in Bob's voice and had been recorded by him at brief, irregular intervals during the weeks immediately following the diagnosis of his illness.

This book is a compilation of those tapes, transcribed pretty much as Bob recorded them. The only changes I have made were those needed to preserve the anonymity of patients and others, and editing to provide transitions and eliminate areas of confusion, unnecessary repetition, and disproportionate length. But that is all. Otherwise, the words that follow are entirely those of Robert Flavin. A name which is, for personal and professional reasons, a pseudonym.

September 24

I'M NOT QUITE SURE what will come of this, Norman. Starting out, the whole idea strikes me as little more than a whim, something to distract myself at a time when I'm very much in need of distraction. I'll simply be talking into a recording device, saying whatever comes to mind on the subject. Which means it will probably be rambling and unscientific at best. Not that I care. I'm not doing this for any psychiatric journal. I'm doing it for myself. And for you. Because it was you, and what I once considered your totally biased opinions on the subject, that first started me thinking about it.

Oh, yes. I haven't yet told you what the subject is,

have I? Well, it happens to be *love*—the love *mystique*—and the unhappy things our scientific and pseudoscientific communities may have done to it.

If you recall, it was you who originally brought up the idea several years ago. In fact you consistently pounded at it in our discussions as well as in your lectures. I remember attacking you once in self-defense. I accused you of pandering to popular prejudices with a lot of half-truths and phony theories, and you responded by telling me to go to hell. Later, I apologized. I always tended to unreasonably harsh judgments of those who consistently beat me in straight sets. Especially when they spouted ideas I didn't agree with in areas in which I believed I had a certain amount of professional expertise. You had a hell of a nerve trying to tell *me*, one of St. Sigmund's holy apostles, anything at all about love. Why you weren't even a *doctor*, for God's sake!

Now, of course, being beyond the help and knowledge of doctors, I'm less inclined to deify the profession. Actually, I never did. If you have the sense you're born with, you very quickly learn how much you don't know.

But first, I must explain about myself. Right after I last saw you at the beginning of September, I became ill with what was later diagnosed as leukemia. I'm not going to bore you with a detailed medical history. Suffice to say, the disease is without a cure and is terminal. The only qualities I can think of in its favor is that it moves quickly and causes little pain. No small things. Although given a choice, I would have preferred it forty or fifty years from now. Still, it's a method of dying which does leave your dignity intact, and I'm grateful for that.

Probably my greatest single reaction is that curious state of disbelief which, against all the facts, makes it impossible to truly accept the idea of your own death. It's a great protection. What the human psyche can't deal with, it simply denies. And having a storehouse of professional knowledge on the subject of dying makes it no easier to experience. I hate it. I despise endings and goodbyes, which is one of the reasons I've avoided getting in touch with you and others who were important to me. I didn't want to have to go through the damned farewells.

Perhaps it comes as a surprise that you were important to me. I know we never spent much time together, but when we did talk, we really talked. You have that rare ability, Norman, to cut through the crap. Most people use words to hide behind. They're afraid of revealing what they feel. You're not. I suppose that's what makes you a writer.

I'm afraid I may be rambling a bit, so please be patient. I'm finding talking to you through this tape a little difficult. I don't know why. If anything, it should be less inhibiting. I can say whatever I choose and not have to care about reactions. One of the few advantages of being terminal. It also makes it easier to add up your profits and losses and strike a final balance, if you're willing to risk the chance of ending up in the red.

I know I called this whole idea a whim before, but that's just not true. I suppose even now I'm trying to protect some remnant of professional pride by implying I don't really take it seriously. Yet I can't imagine anything more serious for me to consider right now. Because a true balance of any life is probably more dependent on an accounting of the love it held or did not hold, than on anything else currently available.

I'm going to personalize this from time to time, Norman. It would be foolish of me to remain above the battle at this stage. I don't think I even want to. But please, if you intend to make any part of these tapes public, I'd appreciate the usual anonymity for all the innocents and not-so-innocents involved.

My earliest memory of what could be considered romantic love began when I was seven years old. The girl's name was Marcella, and although I remained in love with her for three years, we never exchanged a word or touch. I know there are those who wouldn't even dignify this sort of childish crush by calling it love, but I disagree. If anything, the younger we are, the purer the feeling, the less diluted by reason. From the moment Marcella walked into my second grade class, I was gone. Staring at her was like trying to stare at the sun. I had to turn away or go blind. When I didn't see her, I thought about her and this was almost better. What fantasies I built. Nor did I care about not talking to her. How could words possibly add to what I already had? There were other girls with whom I shared words, but I felt nothing for them. Whatever romantic love was in me from ages seven to ten was for Marcella. When she moved away I considered my life over.

The last time I fell in love was just a few years ago. The woman's name was Dorothy, and there was no communication, no touch that we failed to explore. We were like two monkeys happily sitting around picking nits. If a master computer had been programed to pick me the perfect love partner from all available candidates, it could have done no better than Dorothy. And at the end of seven months I was so bored I prayed I'd never have to see her again.

In between Marcella and Dorothy came a fair number of others, all of whom I loved in varying degrees—some briefly, others for longer periods, and a few whom, when I think of them even now, I suppose I still love. One, of course, I actually went so far as to marry, if unsuccessfully. But these are only my personal involvements. It is mostly the perplexity and hurt of my patients' love traumas that have given me the greater share of what I've managed to pick up over the years. We all seem to learn less from our own experiences than from the experiences of others, undoubtedly because we're too emotionally entangled with ourselves to accept what we see.

Still, I did learn that what I had with Marcella as a young schoolboy carried the true mystique of love, and what I had with Dorothy as an experienced adult did not. But that part is relatively simple. Less simple, are the ideas, feelings, and circumstances that brought about such results. And that's what I hope to deal with in these tapes. So stay with me, Norman.

September 25

THERE ARE TIMES, Norman, when I'm absolutely sure that most of what happens to us in the area of love is nothing more than crazy accident. As much as we plan, as much as we make considered judgments, as much as we think we have control over our mating rituals, the results often prove us to be little more than mindless players in a lovers' game of blindman's buff.

When I was a young man, a girl sat beside me on a bus one morning. It was a local Number 3 bus, which I usually didn't ride, but the clutch on my car had died an hour before and I had no other means of transportation. Although the bus was crowded, I found an empty seat beside an elderly man. He left at the next stop and was replaced by a young woman who had just gotten on. She was attractive—not a great knockout, understand—not one of those dazzlers who causes heads to turn, but definitely pretty, with the kind of clean, fresh look I've always liked in women. As she came down the aisle toward me, I remember thinking, cute face, nice breasts, great legs. Those were the pre-perpetual-pants-for-women days, Norman, when you could actually see a girl's legs *before* you went to bed with her.

Anyway, she sat down beside me. And though I'd like to be able to say I picked her up with some fabulous witticism, I'd be lying if I did. All I really managed was to sit silently and stiffly beside her and sneak occasional glances at her breasts in profile. And that was about it, until we both got off at the same corner ten minutes later and I watched those great legs carry her away from me forever. Or so I thought at the time.

But a few days later, Norman, my clutch still being dead, I was on the Number 3 bus again. It was a different bus this time, with a different driver at a slightly different time of day. Still, there she was, coming down the aisle toward me, only this time there were several empty seats available and she didn't choose the one next to me. A definite rejection, I thought. To hell with her. And I didn't even glance in her direction. Yet when we got off together again at the same stop, I got up my courage and approached her with a less than brilliant, "Hi there!"

She wasn't exactly dazzled. She looked at me but didn't stop walking. In fact she didn't even seem to know who I was. "We were on the same bus," I said, trying to make the ten-minute trip sound as though we had shared nothing shorter than a six-month world cruise. She was unimpressed. "*Twice!*" I added for emphasis.

"So?" she said.

Cold, I thought, obviously a very cold type. No warmth, no charm, no personality. Who needed her? Evidently *I* did.

"So," I said, "I was wondering if you'd like to have a drink with me this evening." Then I went for broke. "Or maybe dinner?"

She seemed vaguely astonished. "You mean because we were on a bus together?"

"Twice," I pointed out.

"No, thank you," she said and disappeared into a tall office building and out of my life.

About six months later, a filling had come out of one of my teeth and I was sitting in my dentist's waiting room when I saw her again. She'd evidently had the appointment before me and was leaving. "Hi there," I said. I had learned absolutely nothing in the whole six months.

She looked blankly at me.

"The bus," I said. "*Twice*. Remember?"

"Oh," she said.

"I asked you to have a drink with me."

"And what did I say?" she asked.

"No, thank you."

"How clever of me," she said and started to put on her coat.

A real smart-ass, I thought.

Then the nurse came into the waiting room, and I asked her in to introduce us. She did, and I was at least able to learn her name was Barbara.

Sometime after that—I think it must have been about a year, Norman—I married her.

We were very much in love. Looking at one another, touching, sharing a thousand intimacies, it was hard to imagine ourselves any other way than together.

"I love you," she told me.

"I love you too."

"I never thought I could love anyone the way I love you," she said. "You're so insanely *right* for me."

I told her the feeling was mutual.

"Wouldn't it have been awful if we had never gotten to meet?" she said.

"Awful," I agreed.

"What if I hadn't taken the Number 3 bus at that particular time and on that particular day?" she asked.

"And what if my clutch hadn't died and I hadn't taken the bus at all?"

"And what if that old man hadn't gotten off and left that empty seat beside you?" she said.

"And what if we hadn't gotten on the same bus together the second time?" I asked.

"And what if your filling hadn't fallen out at just that time and forced you to go to the dentist?" she said.

"And what if we hadn't just happened to have the same dentist?" I said.

It was our special love game and we enjoyed playing it. We went through it again and again until it was polished into a minor art form. But it was more than just a game. It was an outlet for our wonder. We knew of no other way to deal with it. We would love one another, raise children together, live, grow old, and die together, and all because of a series of accidents. It frightened us. We didn't want to believe that was the way it really worked. We never mentioned the hand of God because neither of us would admit such a belief. Even the suggestion of some sort of Divine plan would have been embarrassing. We did talk about something called fate once in a while, but always very lightly, always making sure we both knew it was only kidding around.

We also had variations on the Game.

"What made you notice me?" she asked.

"Your breasts and legs," I said.

"What about my face?"

"That was okay," I said, "but your breasts and legs were absolutely super."

"Was that really a sensible basis for wanting to spend a lifetime with me?" she asked.

"I wasn't looking that far ahead," I told her. "I just wanted to get laid."

"That's disgusting."

"No it isn't," I said. "That's the way it works."

She didn't really think it disgusting. She liked the idea of my finding her sexually attractive. But pretending not to was part of it.

"A lot of women have super breasts and legs," she said, "but you don't go around falling in love with them and marrying them."

"You're absolutely right," I agreed. "So I guess you must have had something else that appealed to me."

"It's called a mind."

"Nobody falls in love with a mind," I said. "They might like it, admire it, be stimulated by it, or even be awed by it. But one thing you can be sure they don't ever do is fall in love with it."

"What *was* it then?"

"I don't know," I admitted. "All I do know is that when I wasn't with you, I wanted to be with you. And when I *was* with you, I didn't want to leave you."

"Is that what falling in love is?" she asked.

"I guess for me it is," I said. "That, mixed with a little good, solid lust."

But at the heart of it, Norman, was still the wonder, *and* the confusion, *and* the inability to truly believe that the single most important personal commitment either of us was ever likely to make was based solely on chance. And chance could be cruel, as when Barbara later found she wasn't able to conceive.

"That was the saddest and unluckiest day of your life," she once mourned.

"What day?"

"That day your clutch broke and you took the bus and got involved with and married me, and ended up discovering you were never going to have kids of your own because of me."

She said it like a school girl reciting a memorized lesson. Then she started to cry.

I held her. "Don't talk like that," I said. "I love all broken clutches. I've become a broken-clutch fetishist. I'm forever grateful to broken clutches for you."

"But I can't give you any babies," she wept. "Not *ever.*"

"I didn't fall in love with you and marry you for babies," I said. "I don't even *like* babies, for God's sake!"

"That's not true."

"It's true, it's true," I assured her. "Actually I think I even *hate* babies. I mean they're so small and dumb and they pee and crap in their pants all the time."

She laughed while crying.

"Hey, no fooling," I said. "I never said anything about it before because I was afraid you might hold it against me. Some people even consider it unnatural and un-American to hate babies. You don't know what a relief it is for me to be able to finally come clean about the whole thing."

She dug her fingers into my back. "My God!" she said.

"My God, what?" I asked.

"I love you."

But we weren't about to get rid of the baby problem quite so easily, Norman. Childlessness isn't something that just goes away. It stays. At least it did for my wife. All her friends were either pregnant, talking about being pregnant, or were already diapering. This was before it became acceptable, even fashionable, for a woman actually to *choose* not to have children. In those days a childless married woman was considered, and even considered herself, a freak and an outcast.

"How do you feel about adoption?" Barbara asked one day.

I wasn't surprised by the question, just surprised

that it had been so long in coming. "What's there to feel?" I said. "A baby's a baby."

"Not to some people."

"I'm not some people," I said.

She kissed me. "You never disappoint me."

"Just give me enough time," I said, "and I probably will."

And in time, of course, I did, Norman. As *she* disappointed *me*. As in one way or another we all disappoint.

But in those days, all that was a long way off. We still had the newness and wonder of it. Through a series of crazy accidents, we had come to each other from separate planets. Despite my original snap judgment, she wasn't really a smart-ass, just uncertain and shy. A large part of her wonder was that she couldn't believe I loved her, couldn't believe it was her flesh that drove me wild, her voice I wanted to hear, her laugh that brought me joy. She kept needing reassurances. She had come to me a virgin and in bed she once asked, "How am I?"

"Compared to whom?" I said.

"Everybody."

"I haven't made love to everybody," I said.

"Then those you have."

I considered it. "I'd say you have superb equipment and good instincts," I told her. "The best."

"I don't really do much."

"You don't have to," I said. "A passive woman is often the most exciting."

In that way, Norman, with only love and the best of intentions, I kept her subjugated. But what I had said was true. At that time I did find passive women the most exciting. And her body was pure joy. What an angel of a thing and just waiting to learn!

Young and loving. I loved the way her face looked when I touched her. It was poised, alert. It had an almost daughterly attentiveness. Yet it was wise with an old woman's knowledge. And she always knew what I wanted to hear, even when she was teasing.

"Are all men this wonderful to love?" she asked.

"No," I said. "Most are clumsy, foolish, and inconsiderate."

She sighed. "I feel so selfish, keeping you all to myself."

"All right. Then I'll spread it around."

"You do," she said, "and I'll strangle you." She thought about it. "It's funny, but just thinking about you with another woman makes me a little sick. I never thought I could feel this way, this violently possessive. But then I guess I never loved this way before."

She enjoyed talking about it, Norman. She said she had never imagined how perfect it could be. No one had ever told her—not her mother or her father or the health hygienists at school. Only books had tried to tell her how perfect it could be. But of course books couldn't make her feel it. She said that sometimes it excited her so much thinking about me that she had to touch herself, and this embarrassed her because she had never done it, even as a girl. Other times, when we were together, she found our love making so slow and beautiful that she felt it could last forever. She said I was remaking her, turning her into someone she had never been before, and that I loved her so much she was even beginning to love herself. She was sure there was nobody else on earth who could do this for her, and that we were unique, even sacred together.

Once she was carried away enough to break the rules of the Game. "It wasn't just an accident," she said. "It *couldn't* have been."

"Then what was it?" I asked.

"I don't know," she said. "Maybe there's just no name for it. But I'm sure it was something wonderful and planned, carefully put together by some distant force in some place we know nothing about."

I smiled, but only because I was beginning to feel a bit the same way and it made me comfortable. "You mean someplace like heaven?"

"All right, laugh," she said.

"I'm not laughing."

I had hurt her and made her angry. She had exposed herself in the most private place of all, and I had been less than gracious. I had to make up for it. "I happen to believe it," I said very seriously and carefully.

"What do you believe?"

"That ours was a match made in heaven," I said. "And such being the case, there can be only one logical name for it."

"What's that?" she asked.

"A miracle," I said.

And from that moment on, Norman, my wife and I never referred to our meeting as anything else but The Miracle on the Number 3 Bus.

September 26

WHATEVER MAY HAVE HAPPENED to love and its concepts during this century, Freud was probably responsible for starting most of it.

He was never an especially happy man, and his own love life was no great feast. Sex, for Freud, started late and ended early. After running fitfully between the ages of thirty and forty, it seemed to have dropped out of the race entirely. But that fact had little to do with Freud's professional qualifications. Obstetricians needn't give birth themselves to be certified in their specialty. Sex is just one of love's more sparkling facets, not the whole gem, and this is exactly where much of the confusion lies today.

Of course it all started with the best of purposes. The emotional strictures of the Victorian period were a disaster. Ignorance, guilt, and fear poisoned the bedroom air. A revolution was needed and Freud was the man on the white horse who led it. A flaming emancipator, he drove the libido like a spike into the heart of middle-class prudery. He liberated love from the closet and got sex out from under the sheets. Finally unshackled, Eros danced across millions of newly rumpled beds. Wonderful! A world-wide love revolution led by our Viennese saviour of the couch.

But successful revolutionaries have an unhappy way of becoming new oppressors in their own turn, and many of us who followed Freud were finally no different. Having gotten rid of Victorianism, we established another tyranny to take its place. We practically made the libido a subject of religious worship, with Freud as our Messiah. Having liberated the human race from sexual inhibition and irrational guilt, we put a different breed of monkey on its back. Now everyone had to be a varsity gymnast in bed. All those over twenty-four and unmarried, felt compelled to talk with incredible frankness about their sex lives. Why? Because they were afraid people might otherwise think they didn't have any. And since Freud and all his disciples had revealed how supremely important a role sex played in human psychology, God help anyone caught short there.

You know, Norman, I wouldn't be surprised if we finally arrive at some kind of sexual Olympics. It's not so unreasonable a concept. Society needs yardsticks, a means of measuring things. Score must be kept. How else can we tell who wins? And Eros will finally become too crucial and significant a part of the scene to be kept chained in the bedroom. Love is surely more important than war and athletics. Then why acclaim our military and sports heroes and let our top sex stars blush unseen?

But it's not really that comical. With all our sexual enlightenmen and freedom, there's more impotence and frigidity around today than ever before. There are many reasons, but if I had to pick the single most common one, it would be the current pressure to perform. "Hey, let's *go*, man! How you gonna make the team if you can't do no better'n *that*?" Here's this poor guy trying to make it with a married woman in the front seat of a car and failing miserably. So at the age of thirty-eight he thinks he's impotent and wants to blow his brains out. He's convinced he's supposed to be able to go off like a Roman candle under any and all conditions—and if he isn't able, he's no longer a real man. What he doesn't realize is that he's been conned, that few men could win any sexual blue ribbons while fighting a steering wheel, layers of clothing, the threat of a suddenly materializing husband, and a great clot of guilt over having an affair with another man's wife.

So who conned the guy? I'm afraid Freud gets at least a share of the blame, if not directly, then indirectly, through the exaggerated emphasis on sex encouraged by his theories. And it's not just sex; even our consecrated mother love itself has suffered his cold touch. When have mothers ever felt as guilt-ridden as they do today? Hapless momma doesn't even know what's hit her. All she knows is that she's read somewhere about how psychoanalysis has proved that all her kid's neuroses and failures can be traced back to emotional deprivation in early childhood. Which means it's all her fault; she's failed to do her job properly. Somehow she has failed to grant perfect loving care to her children. She has discovered she's merely human and this is the ultimate sin. Once upon a time, when kids failed or acted up in school, it was considered their own fault and parents beat the tar out of them. Since the advent of Freud and psychoanalysis, parents beat themselves instead.

So with even the best of intentions, we can do damage. We start believing psychoanalysis is a religion whose high priests can do no wrong. Well, we can do plenty of wrong, and much of it comes from pushing into places where we don't belong. Parental love is one of them. Freud comes up with this theory —and mind you, Norman, it's still just a theory— that neurosis is the result of infantile trauma and deprivation, and that it could be prevented by parents loving their children more and caring for them better. Fine. So what happens? On the basis of our own unproved theory, analysts have come to regard themselves as supreme authorities on the raising of children. And we're even accepted by everyone else as authorities. That's about the same as letting an author review his own book.

In the first place, the notion that children should be given plenty of love doesn't require a diploma in psychiatry for its certification. In the second place, the act of loving isn't something we can manage on the advice of doctors or articles. If love is to have any significance at all, it must arise spontaneously and be felt truly. It can't be faked. Finally, much of the trauma suffered by children can't be helped. It's too bad, but that's the way it is. What's the point in insisting that children need their parents' undivided love and attention and shouldn't be separated from them until they reach a certain age, when the facts of life so often make such requirements impossible to fulfill? Parents frequently have an irritating way of dying before their children are old enough to do without their protection and love. There's also no available insurance against parents divorcing one another. Which means that all this wise counseling about children getting proper dosages of parental love is not only gratuitous and perfectionist, but may even cause harm of its own. How? By either pushing parents to be hypocritical, or by making them feel guilty as hell when they may have enough other troubles without adding that to the list. Most parents are decent enough by instinct. They usually do the best they can for their kids within their own and circumstantial limitations. So our psychiatric patients are more likely to be the victims of the calamities of living than of deliberately bad up bringing.

September 27

You knew i was divorced, Norman, but I don't think you knew that both my children were adopted. Not that it was ever a secret. In accordance with all the latest psychological theories, Barbara and I very quickly poured it on the kids themselves and anyone else who would listen. Even before Judi and David were old enough to understand what it was all about, we were busy calling them our *chosen ones* and showering them with more information about adoption than they knew what to do with. The theory being that if they were introduced to the idea early and positively, if they were convinced adoption was good and not merely a second-choice alternative, then they wouldn't be so vulnerable to the negatives. Sounds reasonable, doesn't it? All the experts, all the doctors and psychological counselors think so. And so did I. But not anymore. If I had it to do all over again, Norman, I'd never let my kids know they were adopted. And I'd do everything short of killing to keep anyone else from letting them know.

It's professional heresy, but I don't give a damn *what* the textbooks say. I've lived with this long enough to know there's absolutely no way to make an adopted child feel as well-loved as a natural child. Once he knows he's different, he *feels* different. And different to a child means not as good. We've done a lot of emotional harm in this area. I've done it to my own kids. When they were growing up and needed to feel *most* secure, I made them feel *least* secure. I did it with the best of intentions, but I did it nevertheless. And I saw it happening, step by step, all the classic symptoms. The withdrawal, the alienation, the troubles in school, the gnawing anxiety about their natural parents—the wondering who they were and why they'd rejected them. The whole bit. And finally, that recurrent nightmare of all adoptive parents, that bitter and inevitable accusation, "You're not my *real* father—you can't tell me what to do." I got that too. And don't kid yourself. You may know all about it, but it still hurts.

No. Given another chance, I'd never let them know. I'm very much aware of the dangers in traveling that particular road, but I'd willingly risk it. The worst that could happen would be that later in their lives they might accidentally learn the truth. Which would be a shocker, of course. But they'd be old enough by then to be able to handle it better. And they'd at least have gained the emotional strength and sense of security of growing up in the belief they were no different from their friends.

As medical people, we operate out of textbook and laboratory wisdom and feel so smug in our certainty of being right that we break into a fever if any layman so much as questions us. To admit being wrong would be a suffocation of our faculties. That's how weak our foundations are. And the worst of it is, we all huddle together in this great unholy alliance that we dare to call professional ethics. What a pious misnomer for something that's neither professional nor ethical. A doctor can actually destroy a patient through incompetence, neglect, or sheer stupidity, and remain totally safe from attack by his peers. Amazing, isn't it? Because God help the doctor who violates the code and accuses one of his blood brothers of a professional performance that is anything less than perfect. Before he ever gets another referral, his traitor's tongue will rot and fall out.

So I handled it all wrong with my kids and find small comfort in knowing I did it by the book. I find the entire subject of adoption confusing. It raises too many questions to which we have no answers. Not when it comes to the special kind of love that's involved. And that love *is* special. It's not the same as the love between natural parents and their children. I'm not saying it's better or worse, I'm simply saying it's different. And where I believe that we, as doctors, have demonstrated the worst sort of professional neglect is in not preparing potential adoptive parents for that difference.

The truth is, I was never especially eager about adoption to begin with. I didn't really feel any great need in my life for children. When it became clear that my wife wasn't going to conceive, I would have been just as content to leave it at that. But Barbara had her own needs and I wasn't about to frustrate them, so we adopted. And we were lucky. Though they were two years apart, we got both children as week-old infants, straight from the hospital. What could be better? We had been gifted with sweet, soft, malleable clay, male and female clay, which we would now proceed to mold into our own images. Given love and security from the start, environment would do its good work. We weren't worried about genetics. The kids were physically healthy. There were no noticeable psychoses in their immediate backgrounds. We would love them as our own. What else was there to consider?

Apparently, plenty. Environment didn't play nearly as big a role as I had expected, or maybe, as I had *hoped*. No use fooling myself now. My wife and I were no different from other parents in our ego needs. We instinctively looked for our kids to be little carbon copies of ourselves. But there wasn't a thing we could recognize as part of either of us, so that if love of one's children is indeed a form of self-love, we had no reason for it on that basis. Those two kids just didn't carry any part of us. We had to love them for other reasons, most importantly, for themselves. Which is quite different. It means it doesn't just happen, as it does with your natural son or daughter.

One love is offered free of charge, the other has to be earned. And there's a difference on the negative side as well. When your kid is acting up, when he's demonstrating all of his least appealing traits, you tend to be a lot more tolerant and forgiving if you can recognize those traits as your own, if you can grin and think—just like his old man. Hell! How can I blame *him* if he got it from *me*? But when you're *not* the old man, and the faults are alien and unrecognizable, you're going to be a lot tougher. You're going to wonder—where did the little bastard pick *that* up? It may be a natural enough reaction, but still doesn't stop you from wanting to cut your throat.

The reverse is also true. You're never entirely free of the fear you're being judged the same way, that everything you say and do is being graded on a love scale of one to ten. Does the kid think you don't love him because he's being punished? Does he think you'd act differently if he were your own flesh? And if he does think so, would he be right? You conjure up all sorts of demons. You float between the finger of God and the swish of the Devil's tail. You burn in your own fires. The heat is enormous. But if anything good is ever to come of it, this is where it has to be forged. Because it *can* be good. And when it is good, it's the best.

There have been times, Norman, when I've been in a room with my children and looked at their faces and listened to their voices and known I could never love anything in this world as I loved those two kids.

When you've had to work to get there, when it doesn't come easily and naturally in the usual way, the high points are that much higher. At least that's how it's been for me. I can't say how my children felt about it. My daughter always talked a lot about how much she loved us, but neither of our kids reveal easily, and they're especially closed with me because of my work. There's an irony in that, of course. I deal professionally with the emotions, so my own are immediately suspect. "You've got to watch out how you talk to daddy. Be careful what you say. You know how shrinks are." Everything out of your mouth means something on two levels.

But I hope they've been able to feel love for me. I can't imagine anything sadder if they haven't. I mean, for them, though I haven't always been immune to bitter moments of my own. Ungrateful kids, I'd think, then laugh at myself for thinking it. I should know better. I'm trained to know better. You can't love out of gratitude. Love is not a way of saying thanks. We may sometimes try to use it that way but it never works, and this is where parents are especially guilty. We think we can issue love to our kids like so many promissory notes, then collect on them when they fall due. In this, at least, all parents are the same, natural and adoptive. "After all I've done!" has become our universal cry of martyrdom. Yet what have we done, really, other than allow ourselves the privilege and joy of loving?

Still, it's easier to blame psychiatry than myself in these things. Wasn't Freud the well spring of it all? I was just a loyal follower. And one of the many gardens of arrogance into which he led us was that of pedantic smugness. God, can we be smug! We have it systematized.

First, we establish the doctrine that neurosis is caused by lack of love in childhood. Then, of course, we accuse Mommy and Daddy of being the ones who messed things up. Parental deprivation is the name we give it. After which we state that analysis is the needed form of replacement therapy, and the most important element in that treatment is the doctor's devotion and love. But what we manage to leave curiously unexplained is why our pompous Freudian shock troops, the practicing analysts, should consider themselves as possessing greater stores of love than their patients' parents. That is not only the ultimate in *chutzpah*, but an utterly unjustified claim to moral superiority over the laity. Listen to us, we say, and we'll cure whatever ails you because we love you more than your own mother and father.

But we didn't *really* love them. What we did, mostly, was engage in a little educated play-acting at about fifty dollars per forty-five minute hour. And those who listened to us weren't always cured. And of those who were cured, there was often a good number whom we somehow managed to infect with alternative diseases. Naturally it wasn't deliberate. But that didn't always prevent our cures from resulting in more painful damage than the disorders they were meant to heal.

I admit to a fair share of those myself, although most were limited to my early practice. I like to believe I was at least able to learn as I went along, which is why we call our work a practice. That's exactly what we do—*practice*. And if we're smart and lucky, we may finally get it right more often than wrong.

So at the beginning, Norman, I'm afraid I tended to get it less right than at the end. Not that it ever becomes easy, simple, or certain. When you're dealing with the emotions, it's like trying to drive through fog. Everything is amorphous and changing. Nothing is clearly defined. Even when you know where you're going, you can't be sure of getting there. And if you do get there, you don't always know it. God, how I've envied surgeons at times. What a luxury to be able to make an incision with the sharp, clean edge of a scalpel, see your problem lying exposed, do whatever you have to do, and know definitely within hours or days how effective you've been. At best, I've had to be satisfied with a vague hope. At worst, I've felt helpless and inept. In between, I've stumbled towards occasional patches of light. And through the years, this was what I've felt pleased to consider the practice of psychiatry.

September 29

As I SAID, it was during my early years of practice that I made some of my worst mistakes. Of course I didn't consider them mistakes at the time, and there are many analysts who still wouldn't. But *I* do. And prominent among my mistakes was Sheila Miller.

Sheila was about thirty-five when she first came to me as a patient. She was well educated, had two young children, and was married to an aggressive, not especially sensitive man whom she loved very much. Her family doctor had suggested psychiatric help after she became depressed, lost weight, stopped doing her housework and spent an inordinate amount of time staring at nothing. Although I didn't consider her suicidal, she did occasionally say she thought everyone might be better off if she weren't around. I tried an antidepressant drug on her, but it didn't work. These drugs seem to work in about seventy percent of the cases and are worthless for the rest. Nobody knows why they work for some and not for others, nor do we really know why shock treatment is effective only for some. However, we do have a lot of theories about the advantages of psychotherapy, although few of us agree on any single one. But psychotherapy was what I chose to go into with Sheila.

It turned out to be long, deep, and hard. Even when she was well, Sheila rarely projected joy. She did laugh a great deal, but it was mostly a nervous giggle. At best, she was an insecure person whose parents had sat heavily on her and done a good job of making her feel inadequate. Then her husband came along and they fell in love and married. He adored her gentleness and passivity. He was one of those burly, domineering types who consider these traits the ultimate in femininity. For her part, Sheila leaned on his strength and self-reliance. Whatever their psychological problems, there was no doubt that they loved one another.

But love wasn't what I was being called on to deal with. My main objective was Sheila's depression. I had to make a more confident, assertive person out of her. It wasn't easy. What her parents had started, her husband had finished. But I ploughed ahead and after more than a year of therapy, Sheila was showing more confidence than she had ever shown in her life. She was even able to express opinions that differed from those of her husband. And this was exactly where the complications began.

I wasn't at all surprised. I knew her husband wasn't going to be crazy about the new Sheila. I knew he would have to make an adjustment, but I also knew he wasn't likely to be able to make it. This kind of man rarely can. Not that he didn't try. On my advice, he actually went so far as to enter therapy himself, with another doctor. But he couldn't take it and soon quit. At this point the Millers' marriage began coming apart. With Sheila no longer the passive darling that Frank had fallen in love with, there was almost constant bickering. All of which Sheila reported to me in detail, like a general sending communiqués from the front. While I, naturally, bolstered her forces and fed her more ammunition. I was strictly partisan. My job was to turn her into a more positive human being, which would, in turn, alleviate her depression and allow her to function normally. And I was accomplishing my purposes. Never mind that I was also destroying the love that had held her marriage together for ten years. First things first. There would be time enough later to deal with a rebelling husband and disintegrating marriage.

But there wasn't time. Somehow, Frank Miller wasn't tuned in on my game plan. He didn't like anything about the new wife I had given him. By his standards she had become tough, opinionated, argumentative, and totally self-absorbed. And compared with the guilt-ridden, obsequious mouse she had once been, Sheila undoubtedly did seem all these things to him. So one day Frank left her and sued for divorce.

He just didn't want to live with the new Sheila. It did little good to point out that she was still the same woman he had married, that she loved him as much as ever, that having opinions different from his didn't mean she respected or cared for him any less. He wanted no part of her.

Too bad, I thought, but you can't have it all ways. The important thing was my patient, and she was doing fine. But not for long.

With her husband gone, everything I had carefully built, all that beautiful confidence collapsed like a rotted building. Sheila had a complete mental breakdown and had to be hospitalized. Her parents removed me from the case and I lost track of her. But about a year later I saw an old picture of her in a newspaper. The picture must have been taken when she was in college. She was laughing and the sun was shining on her long blond hair and she looked absolutely lovely. The article under her picture said that she and her two children had died in a gas explosion and fire that started in their kitchen. A partially burned letter to her husband was found in an upstairs bedroom. It was a suicide note.

Frank Miller came to see me a few days after it happened. He came to my house late one night, and when I saw him at the door, I was scared stiff. The threat of violence from patients or their relatives is a recurrent nightmare of psychiatrists. But whatever black mood Miller was in, it was controlled. He simply accused me of murdering his wife and children. He said I had killed them as surely as if I had turned on the oven myself and set a match to it. He admitted to some blame himself. He knew it wouldn't have happened if he hadn't walked out on her. But he hammered me with most of it for turning his wife into the kind of woman he couldn't live with. And as far as he went, he was right.

Oh, I know all the proper answers and denials. We have textbooks filled with them. Any professional review board would have judged my procedures correct. And at that time, so did I. But not anymore. With the beautiful lucidity of hindsight, I can now see what I couldn't or wouldn't see before. And that's the importance of the love factor, which would have made me handle things very differently.

I concentrated too much on just Sheila. Although she was my patient and her problems were severe ones, I should have compromised in my treatment. I knew what sort of man her husband was. I knew he wasn't likely to accept a wife who stood up to him, that there was a good chance he might leave her. But I was turning out a beautiful product, a fine, new, confident Sheila, and I was so proud of it that I was willing to gamble on making her strong enough to survive even a possible broken marriage. And I had no right to take that gamble. It was too much of a risk, too dangerous. And events finally proved it so.

Whatever their imperfections, those two did care about one another. And there's small satisfaction in being able to call Frank an insensitive, domineering, male-chauvinist lout. But I should have considered that in treating his wife. I should have weighed the importance of Sheila's need for him, and I didn't, at least not enough to change my procedures. I should have known it was as important to hold those two people together as it was to rid my patient of her depression. But it was apparently against my religion. The litany was clear. My duty was to bolster Sheila's sagging libido, not her marriage. I was a doctor, damn it, not a marriage counselor. So I doctored a woman and two children into early graves and had the doubtful solace of knowing my medical procedures were one hundred percent correct.

Sheila Miller was undoubtedly my most tragic mistake in this area, but she wasn't my only one. If you believe something strongly enough, and have enough experts to back you up, you can somehow manage to avoid learning anything at all from experience. God knows how many marriages I helped dissolve while firming up sagging psyches. Where love may still have been able to limp along *before* I was called in, it was sure to fall flat on its face soon *after*. You could depend on it. Divorce lawyers should have adored me. How those lawyers prospered because of me. And how love suffered.

October 1

I'M FEELING A BIT WEAKER TODAY, Norman. Though
it's not too bad. It comes and goes. But when I'm
like this, it's hard for me to imagine I was ever any
other way. That's what can be so depressing about
this whole business. I'm afraid I might finally forget
the good and be left only with this.

I've never talked much about myself to anyone
before. Even this taping was intended more as a
polemic than a confessional. Or at least I thought it
was. Obviously I was wrong, because I'm sticking
myself into it more and more. There's something
seductive about a microphone. It's so marvelously
patient and it doesn't talk back. Like a good psy-

chiatrist, maybe even better. At least it doesn't cut you off after forty-five minutes and send you away just when the juices are flowing well. Nor does it bill you at the end of the month.

But in my mind I'm talking to *you*, Norman, not the microphone. You see, we do need someone human at the other end. And in a very real sense, I'm putting a weight on you. Forgive me for not asking your permission or at least warning you. I guess I took it for granted you wouldn't mind. Anyway, for you to understand some of my attitudes and prejudices, it might help to know a little about my background.

To begin with, there's the fact of my being Jewish. Never mind that I haven't been inside a synagogue in thirty years. You don't have to pray in order to be Jewish. Nor can you escape five thousand years of blood and tradition by calling yourself an agnostic, a Unitarian, or anything else. It's the one thing the Nazis seem to have understood. A Jew is a Jew is a Jew. And my being a doctor doesn't change that, because beneath it all, beneath education and training and forty-two years of living, still lies the Jewish mystique and its inalterable effect on everything I touch.

With love, it starts early. Almost as soon as we learn we're divided into boys and girls, we learn that girls are divided into Jewish girls and *shiksas*, the kosher and nonkosher, the acceptable and forbidden. The Jewish girls, of course, are dark-haired, brown-eyed, intelligent, supremely moral, and dedicated to marriage and motherhood. The *shiksas* are yellow-haired, blue-eyed, dumb—until I started school I thought *dumb shiksa* was one word—without morals and placed on earth solely for Jewish boys to lust after but never take seriously. So naturally the first girl I fell totally in love with, my Marcella, was the archetypical blonde, blue-eyed *shiksa.*

It occurs that St. Sigmund was also Jewish. As was Wilhelm Reich. As is Erich Fromm. So what about *their* Jewishness and its effect on our current psychoanalytic approach to love? Surely it must be considerable. Isn't there something ironic in *that?* The idea of this tiny cabal of Jewish doctors, representing a religious group that constitutes less than one percent of the world's population, so strongly influencing western civilization's reigning psychological concepts of love is really very funny. If love is indeed in trouble these days, we may have inadvertently given the anti-Semites their quintessential reason for being. Now we'd be the love-killers. After almost two thousand years we still haven't convinced them we didn't murder Christ, and now we'd have this.

Let's look at it a minute. Among Western cultures, we Jews have always been unique in our attitudes towards love and sex. Since learning and the intellect have traditionally been our most serious devotions, the body and its appetites were considered little more than dangerous distractions. Sex was needed for procreation, but it could be disruptive if not satisfied. The damn thing got in the *way.* A Talmudic student with an erection was worthless. There's an old Yiddish saying: *"Ven der petzel steht, der sechel geht."* When the penis stands, sense goes. The poor thing was regarded as a second-class citizen, a poor country cousin to the mind. It had to be kept pacified or else it would bring trouble and disgrace. And the only acceptable way to keep it appeased was through marriage.

Which meant that other than for its part in continuing the family line, sex was regarded as pretty much of a nuisance. In fact traditionalist Jews made love almost as if it were a ritual, with time, place, and manner dictated by custom. Spontaneity was nonexistent. Love wasn't supposed to be something romantically longed for or fulfilling in itself. That would be utter foolishness. And as far as the pure joy of it was concerned, you could forget it. *What* joy? Joy for the true Jew was in intellectual exaltation, in wit, argument, and learning. You didn't use sex for fun. The body was no playground. Unbridled sex and romantic love were looked upon as Christian inventions. And apart from everything else, they were luxuries the Jews couldn't afford while worrying about survival and God's approval. Just observing their religious rituals was a full-time job. Love as a moral question was fine, but as an emotional passion you avoided it. It was bondage of the worst sort.

So here we are, an historically joyless, moral people, somehow charged with setting up many of the rules for the big love sweepstakes. Which is pretty much like putting a bunch of Temperance Leaguers in charge of the agenda for the National Distillers Convention. And there's no doubt that we've had our effect on it. As intellectuals, we've stolen much of the mystery from love and replaced it with reason. We're very big on explaining. Nothing must be left unclarified. We must understand everything. And if we can't understand everything, it's important to pretend we do. One of the worst things a Jew could say about his beloved is, "I love her, but I don't know why." God forbid he should ever admit such a thing. If he doesn't know, he'd damn well better be able to make something up for himself. And fast. Otherwise, love will very soon be gone.

I didn't always know this. I was lucky at the beginning. I was a very unintellectual type of Jewish kid. I read little, and what I did read I quickly forgot. Mostly, I just stumbled about in the garden of love, considering it the true Eden, only better, because I thought this one had no snakes. And what fantasies I had! What beautiful things I imagined. I can't remember how close to reality my dreams actually came, but that doesn't matter. At least I had my chance at visions. I was able to close my eyes and let my mind roam. Love may not have to be blind to be good, but it does help if it's a little myopic. So I was also lucky to have done most of my sexual growing up before Kinsey and Masters and Johnson and the rest of our current crop of sex excavators came along with their shovels and microscopes and syndromes of total reality. Because there's nothing erotic about complete realism. And this is precisely where the medical sex excavators made their most serious mistakes in formulating their manuals.

I remember what happened to me as a young intern. Suddenly my world seemed filled with naked female bodies. I mean living ones, not cadavers. Some were less than lovely, but others were beautiful by any standards. And I'd look at them under the cold hospital lights and consider their female parts and feel nothing that a young male of the same species should feel. But then I'd leave the hospital and go out into the street where I'd see no more than three inches of exposed thigh as some passing girl stepped into a taxi, and everything changed. My head swiveled, my eyes popped, my palms grew moist, and I'd stand staring after the cab with regretful hunger as it and the girl disappeared.

The entire incident might have lasted no more than thirty seconds, but as I walked on, my fantasies took over. I imagined what the rest of the girl's body was like. From those three briefly viewed inches of thigh, I mentally constructed flesh, fragrance, and feel. I heard the girl's voice, the way she spoke, the sweetness of what she said. And everything was exactly to my taste. Why not? Since I was creating this erotic vision entirely for myself, who else did I have to please? I had bred and fashioned total love from a tiny scrap of flesh. And the girl was beautiful, though I hadn't seen any part of her face. Or maybe that was *why* she was beautiful. Having seen nothing, there was nothing to displease me. And what reality could match *that*?

All of which may sound a bit cynical, Norman, but it's not. I'm too much of a romantic to be cynical. Not that I'm different from you or anyone else. In one way or another we're all romantics, and looks, age, and background have little to do with it.

A few years ago, a neighbor of mine, Ralph Shapiro, a middle-aged Great Neck dentist, left his wife of thirty-two years and trotted off to California with his twenty-five-year-old nurse. You should have heard the screaming from the other wives on that block. Their husbands all wore sly little grins, but the women were furious. "The nerve of him!" they wailed. "That miserable little shrimp. Look at him! Fifty-four years old, fat, bald, and five-foot-nothing. How *dare* he? Who does he think he is? *Robert Redford?*"

Their anger was understandable. They were frightened. This was hitting too close to home. It was all right for those distant, glamorous movie actors and jet-setters to leave their wives for cute young chicks. They all enjoyed reading about that. But Ralph Shapiro was something else. He wasn't that far removed from their own husbands. If he could do something like that to his wife, then none of them was safe. So the neighborhood's once secure wives looked at their aging husbands a bit differently and railed at the nerve of Ralph Shapiro, who was middle-aged and physically unattractive and must have had this crazy idea that he was Robert Redford.

What they failed to understand was that *inside*, Ralph *was* Robert Redford. Inside, he was young and handsome and irrepressibly romantic. Which is pretty much the way we all are. Our packaging may vary and fade, but that rarely affects the way we feel. And the idea that a man must be young, tall, slender, and handsome in order to qualify for romantic longings, is just one more Hollywood-inspired illusion. Women are no different. Inside, they remain perennial ingénues. It's one of nature's less kind little tricks. Still feeling like eighteen, we look into our mirrors, see these aging strangers staring back at us and think it's some sort of nightmarish mistake. But it's not. It's no mistake. And we all have our own ways of dealing with it. Little Ralph Shapiro's way was to take off with his twenty-five-year-old nurse.

The sex excavators are no help. If anything, they just make it worse. They pour out their reams of statistics and case histories and act as though factual knowledge in itself was a cure-all. Well, it doesn't cure a thing. To discover that our real, personal longings have been given the medical titles of syndromes or neuroses or particular patterns of behavior offers absolutely no comfort. It's a denial of everything we feel. It makes us desperate to establish our own identity, to prove we're different, not just another statistic.

Ralph Shapiro wasn't a patient of mine, but he didn't have to be for me to know his lament. "Listen to me!" was his cry. "I'm fifty-four years old and my contemporaries are starting to appear on the obituary pages. I work twelve hours a day, make a lot of money, and find neither work nor money very important anymore. I'm a bald, fat, aging little man whose wife values him somewhere between her Mercedes and her house furnishings, and whose children consider him vaguely amusing and archaic when he gives them what they want, and a chintzy old bastard when he doesn't. My wife hasn't initiated a sexual advance towards me in twenty years and does little more than tolerate mine. I think if I never approached her in bed again, she'd be relieved. Which means she either has a lover, has lost all sexual desire, or prefers masturbation to me. And frankly, I don't care. She's no longer exciting to me anyway. When I do make love to her, it's like masturbating with a partner. She feels nothing and neither do I. So, what the hell. What am I giving up? A long, slow, dull slide into old age and death? I've decided that's not the way I want it. Not if I can help it. And if it takes a girl half my age to change things, I'm willing to try that too. I may not be any prize, but at least she makes me feel like one. She *wants* me, for God's sake! When we're alone, she can't keep her hands off me. Imagine! Fat old Ralph Shapiro, a sex object. Everyone tries to give me reasons. They try to spoil it. They tell me she's just after my money, that she needs a father figure, that she's a silly young fool with whom I won't find a thing to talk about. Well, to hell with them all. I don't give a damn what her needs are. Let her *have* my money. Let me *be* her father figure. And I've already had enough talk to last the rest of my life. This woman makes me *feel* again and that's all I care about."

Shapiro's lament. Though it's really less a lament than a shout of affirmation. And he's not alone. There are more voices of Shapiro than of turtles heard in the land today. And how do most shrinks and sex excavators deal with their problem? At best, simplistically, at worst, destructively.

First, we give it labels. We call it male menopause, or death syndrome, or age complex, or whatever. Then we draw a few more buckets of statistics from our bottomless wells to prove the authenticity of our labels. Then we pat all the little Shapiros patronizingly on their heads and assure them that they're not especially unique, that there are countless other middle-aged men going through the same things and suffering the same symptoms, that given time and understanding, the necessary adjustments to age will take place, it will all pass, and they will resume their proper positions and responsibilities in the general scheme of things.

Well, the Shapiros of the world don't *want* to hear that what they're feeling is nothing but a damn medical symptom. They don't *want* to be told that they're not especially unique, that there are countless others just like them. In fact, they find such a concept utterly horrifying. It smothers whatever tiny flame of ego still survives. It makes the love they're just beginning to feel banal, makes it seem less than ordinary. At any age one of the true wonders of love is its ability to transcend all logic, to convince us somehow that what we're lucky enough to have, no one has ever quite had before. And the older we are, the deeper the sensation, the more precious the delight. Our Shapiros aren't new to the feast, Norman; they're not just nibbling at the appetizer. They've reached the dessert. They're at the end and they know it's the last course for them. So they eat slowly, deliciously, savoring each bite and trying to shut their ears to the medical Cassandras wailing of indigestion ahead.

And they certainly don't want to hear that it's all going to pass and that they'll be back where they were before. But sometimes they do go back. Sometimes the doctors and the statistics get to them, and they lose heart or courage or whatever it was that gave them the incentive to make their move in the first place.

Ralph Shapiro was one of those who went back. The joy was apparently too much for him. His Jewish morality couldn't stand the idea of so much pleasure. He missed the abuse he used to receive from his wife and children. There are such people, you know. Unless they're hurting, they think something is wrong. So seven months after he left, Ralph returned home, bent his head, and apologized to his wife for his effrontery. The housewives of Great Neck rejoiced and felt secure once more. The aging husbands of Great Neck sighed. Shapiro was no longer Robert Redford. He was a fat little middle-aged dentist, back in his proper place.

Actually, it was his wife's doctor who got him back, a sixty-buck-an-hour shrink, complete with Prince Valiant haircomb and Pierre Cardin suits. All right. So I admit to a petty prejudice against alleged men of science who preen and feather themselves like those wax dummies who read the news on television. Anyway, this psychiatric glamour boy managed to let Ralph know that his wife had developed clear-cut suicidal tendencies, and that if he didn't hustle his fat little ass back where it belonged, he might have to live out his days with tragedy on his conscience. Which is the ultimate in medical blackmail; although there are no actual laws against it, and it's practiced more often than you can imagine. Not that it took very much outside pressure to get Ralph home. He had enough of his own innate masochism going to give him a good start in that direction. But it was the shrink's blackmail by innuendo, that provided the little extra push he needed.

I'm not sure what happened to his woman. The last I heard, she was still somewhere in California, undoubtedly living well on the generous cash settlement it was in Ralph's nature to apply as a pain-killer. I'm not at all worried about her. I'm sure she'll do well enough. It's Ralph who saddens me when I think of him, with his little love dream quietly fading and Robert Redford put to sleep forever.

I wonder what goes on inside him in the early evening quiet, when his work is done and the radio music drifts softly. Does he think of his woman then and the particular way she looked and spoke? I think I would. I do, even now, when I know I'll never physically love again, when my body has totally stopped being my own. I do think such thoughts.

October 4

AN INTERESTING FACT, Norman: I've discovered an odd similarity between sexual pleasure and extreme physical pain. And it has nothing to do with the sadomasochistic bit. What I mean is that despite their intensity, despite their unequaled power over mind and body while you're experiencing them, when they're over you can't really remember what they felt like. Which is fine as regards the pain, but not so great about the love. So in my mind, at least, I'll die a virgin. We apparently go out as innocent in that area as we entered. If not intellectually, then at least in feeling. I can remember everything I ever did in bed, but nothing at all of how it felt doing it.

Yet I do recall the peripheral sensations of the act of love, the feelings which, at the good moments, surrounded the physical. I once took walks in the park with a girl I loved. I used to meet her in the late afternoon, and sometimes when I arrived she'd be waiting and I'd see her sitting by the lake, the sun on her hair and her head bent in a special little way she had, and I swear it was enough to break my heart just to look at her. Our lovemaking was equally lovely, but it isn't the touch of her flesh that I remember now. It's what I felt when I saw her there in the sun. *That's* what has hung on all these years.

People who don't know, who have never experienced it, or for one reason or another, can't understand what it's all about tend to dismiss such things as sentiment. They call it romanticizing, as if this in itself were some sort of emotional treason. And allied with them are the sex excavators, with Masters and Johnson marching way out in front, banners high, their sexual war declared, the laboratory their arsenal and total realism their rallying cry. Which isn't entirely bad, of course. In fact there was something quite positive, for one thing, in getting the good word across that masturbation didn't really make you crazy and blind. But conversely, I wonder how much good will be achieved in male-female relations by the recently publicized results of their most famous experiments, which contended, among other things, that a woman can achieve a far more intense orgasm alone, through her own efforts, than she can with the most capable male partner.

Now isn't that a great piece of news? Isn't it nice

to know your woman doesn't really need you and your breathless, sweaty little body after all, that she probably just keeps you in bed for laughs and someone to talk to? Doesn't that laboratory-inspired bit of reality do marvelous things for your libido? No one is ever likely to accuse the scientific team of Masters and Johnson of foolish romanticizing. They are two doctors who clearly know where the act of love is at. And where it is currently at for them, is on a clean white laboratory table, with electrodes attached to all the necessary parts, a dozen lights flashing, and plastic vibrators shimmying for all they're worth. What a love dream!

What bothers me most is the aura of authenticity that surrounds anything that seems the least bit scientific. There's no sound of laughter in the laboratory. There's only the ring of indisputable truths. And the fact that in a few weeks, months, or years, a totally new set of indisputable truths may well replace the current crop is rarely considered by the layman. This is the era, in human history, of the doctor as God. It's a time-tested formula. Reverence plus money equals infallibility. Only we happen to be very fallible. Even in the sacred halls of our laboratories.

Consider the conditions, Norman, under which our revered sex excavators had to come up with their great, masturbatory breakthrough. Consider the problems they faced before they could even begin.

First, they had to find subjects, people, men and women, who would not only be willing to take part in so patently humiliating an exercise, but who would be physically able to perform as required. Second, they had to establish an entirely new system of controls, of checks and balances that would conform to laboratory standards. And third, they had to create a satisfactory means of measuring the intensity of the female orgasm, one that would be scientifically indisputable and not subject to the vagaries of human judgment.

It had to take a very special breed of woman to be willing even to volunteer for this sort of experiment. Not only was she being called upon to masturbate and have sexual intercourse before an audience of strangers, but while all this was going on, she had to suffer being hooked up internally and externally to a gaggle of electronic devices that would monitor and record every sigh, quiver, gasp, scream, moan and impulse, every twitch, gush, lunge, and dilation. So who would be likely to volunteer? Our so-called average housewife? The girl nextdoor with her romantic illusions intact? The reasonably modest woman who has probably been loved by no more than an average of one and a half men in the course of her lifetime—and these in quiet, solitary splendor? Hardly.

The volunteers for this kind of gig are most likely to be hookers in it for the money, kooks who will try anything for kicks, pseudo-intellectual hop-sackers who find something oddly stimulating in the idea of spreading their legs for science, and the group sexists who aren't turned on at all anymore unless they have a fair-sized crowd watching. And it's from this allegedly representative group of female volunteers that scientific judgments have been made and conclusions reached that are supposed to be indicative of the responses of all womankind.

Then we come to the responses themselves: the levels of pleasure, the intensities of passion as measured by the cold electronic eyes of the machines. You can imagine how relaxing it must have been, how spontaneous and joyful, to make love under such circumstances. It's a wonder that all senses weren't paralyzed, a miracle that those pathetic guinea pigs under the lights were able to feel *anything*, with this battery of eminent experts leaning over them, perhaps encouraging and cheering them on like fans at a racetrack.

I've wondered about that part, Norman. Did the sex experts ever take sides in the contest? Or did they demonstrate a properly scientific lack of bias? There's no way of knowing, of course, but my own feeling is that they were probably hoping that masturbation would be wearing the roses in the winner's circle. It was such a really long shot and who doesn't love to see a long shot come in? Besides, what sort of big splash would it have made to announce that sex was better for a woman with a man in attendance than alone? It would have been like announcing that sex had been discovered to be more fun than croquet.

But turn it around the other way and give them the unexpected, and trumpets would sound. Men would at last be expendable in the most crucial area of all. What a boost for women's liberation. Females would finally be freed of their historical serfdom to the phallus. It would be the dawn of a whole new era in human sexuality. And with so much at stake, there might even be a temptation to fix the race.

Not that I'm making any such accusation. It's not the integrity of the good doctors that I'm questioning in this particular case, but the value of their results. Apart from everything else, the entire concept is just too destructive—not only to the future of the human male as a desired sex partner, but to me personally.

Damn it, Norman! I refuse to die believing that whatever pleasures I may have contributed in bed, were but a poor substitute for milady's finger. That's just too bitter a dose to take with me. I prefer to believe that through the years, in my own modest way, I did manage to offer something more than mere companionship and conversation in the bedroom, that the small cries of joy I may have heard were not simply lies or the result of a reluctantly accepted alternative, and that the romantic dreams they inspired had more to do with the true meaning of love than all the alleged realities of the world's sex labs lumped together.

October 5

I'VE FOUND THAT when people speak of love, Norman, they often have sad eyes. Even when they're
happy, their eyes seem to be preparing for hurt. I
suppose it's a kind of protection we use. We find it
hard to trust what's ahead. Don't get yourself too
worked up, say the eyes; don't be too happy about
your love because it's not going to last. You're going
to lose it. In one way or another, it ends. Which is
true. Love *is* terminal. Sooner or later one of you,
either you or your love, changes, fades, goes away, or
dies. And apparently the eyes know it.

I've seen a lot of such eyes over the years. Among
the saddest of them all, were the eyes of a patient

named Victor Kazinski. Which was a bit unusual, because Victor's eyes were a pale cornflower blue and it's never easy for such eyes to be sad.

Victor was a tall, fair-haired man with great hands who worked as a skilled machinist. The son of a Polish immigrant, he had a fine job, brought home a generous salary and took a quiet but strong pride in the fact that he had gone to school and achieved the education and skills that lifted him above the average worker. It was the kind of very specific, old-fashioned male pride—call it chauvinist if you will—that said these were the things that labeled him a man, marked him the head of his family, and made him worthy of respect. His wife worked too and earned good pay as a bookkeeper for an automobile dealer. But this was no threat. Victor was secure enough in his own achievements. Also, there was love. The Kazinskis had as good a marriage as you're likely to see around.

Then one day the company where Victor had worked for fourteen years went out of business and he was out of a job. For the first time in his adult life, he had no place specific to go in the morning and nothing productive to do. It hit him like a kick in the gut. Because there was a general recession in the aerospace industry, Victor's specialty, no other jobs were available. He sat at home and looked at the walls, and all the things that can happen to a man under such conditions began happening to him. There were no immediate money problems. He had his savings, his wife was still working, and unemployment checks and union benefits were coming in. But Victor gradually began feeling like less of a man. Good God, he thought. I, Victor Kazinski, can no longer support my wife and family. And riding the thought like a demon in a nightmare, came its companion—impotence. Suddenly, Victor found himself unable to make love to his wife.

Impotence can be a frightful affliction for any man, but do you have any idea, Norman, what a special horror it is for someone with Victor Kazinski's values? Because he was ashamed to reveal his problem to anyone, he tried to treat it himself. He not only read stacks of sex manuals, but experimented with techniques and treatments culled out of everything from Zen Buddhist and Hindu sex rites to the latest in Haitian voodoo. He forced his poor wife to do everything but hang upside down from the ceiling with him, and nothing helped. There was still a deadness in his loins and it was beginning to work its way into his heart. Hating himself, he began hating his wife as well. *He* was at home and *she* was out there working. *He* was nothing and *she* was the man of the family. With others he was silent and angry. With her he shouted, trying to make noises like a man. Alone, he wept, wishing himself dead. How did such a thing happen to a man? What great sin had he committed to have drawn so terrible a vengeance from God?

In desperation, he finally agreed to allow the dread secret out of his house. Together, he and his equally suffering wife enrolled in a sex clinic. Things were done to them. They did things to each other and to themselves. They listened to lectures, watched films, looked at pictures, read books, memorized pamphlets. They fondled, tickled, stroked, and caressed. They did it by daylight, lamplight, and in darkness. They undressed, dressed, and partially dressed themselves and each other. They sighed, screamed, gurgled and gasped, and did everything they were told to do by a team of experts. They did it for two solid weeks in a locked motel room in a strange and distant city and at the end of that period were forced to carry home Victor's manhood in as flaccid and lifeless a state as it had arrived.

Victor came to me as a patient about a year later. By this time his marriage had gone to pieces and he had left his wife and children. Facing them on a daily basis had finally proved too much. And he looked at me with those sad cornflower blue eyes, the love, hurt, and confusion all jumbled there together, and asked me why, if God were truly kind, He didn't just kill him quickly if he had done something wrong and not slowly torture him to bits this way.

I confessed to being fairly ignorant of God's reasoning, but said I was sure his sexual troubles would be over as soon as he found a job. It wasn't nearly as simple as all that, of course, but that was basically it. To Victor, it was all academic anyway, since he saw little hope of finding a job. But since I had already cast myself in the role of prophet, I saw no harm in playing a bit of God as well. I asked around among some contractors I knew and was lucky enough to find one with an opening to match Victor's skills. And I hadn't been wrong. The job came with a bona fide erection attached.

I had to fight Victor off. He wanted to kiss my hands, my feet, my face, my lips. Leave me alone, I told him. Never mind about me. Just put that thing to work where it will be properly appreciated. He went back to his wife. But not right away. He wanted a bit of practice first on the outside. He wanted to be sure he could handle it all right. It had been a long time for him. "But you don't really forget," he told me. "I guess it's like swimming or driving a car. You never really forget."

So you see, Norman, I didn't always do so badly with my patients in the area of love. Sometimes other doctors, other experts did badly with them before they came to me, and I had to try to fix them up. In Victor Kazinski's case, it was the sex clinic and the manuals that did him wrong. Perhaps that's a trifle unjust, inasmuch as his problem did start well in advance of his using them. But since their treatments and advice were useless, they were also dangerous. They caused valuable time to be lost during a most destructive period. Irreparable harm might have been done to the lives of the members of an entire family in that year and a half. Probably, harm *was* done. The scars of such wounds often show up many years later.

But the major trouble with most of these sex clinics—and especially in cases like Victor's—is that they treat problems too simplistically. They tend to leave out all the social experiences, all the emotional complications that so often tie into what appears to be a purely sexual problem. And that's the worst part of it. When there's a sexual malfunction, it's rarely just a physical thing. Victor wasn't impotent because something was wrong with his body or his and his wife's love-making techniques. His trouble was up-stairs in his brain, in whatever part of that maze of tiny compartments that exists to deal with male pride.

The sex clinics generally ignore the full human equation involved in the act of love and concentrate solely on the genitals. Which can be a disaster. Sex is psychological and sociological as much as it is bio-logical, and it's this entire combination of elements that can't help but affect our love lives. Yet those who run these sex spas, whether they be professionals, paraprofessionals or simply enthusiastic amateurs, are too often so preoccupied with the physical aspects of sex, with its pure mechanics and technology, that they ignore the total substance of love. And a large num-ber of the love cripples that have limped through my office over the years are living examples of the de-struction that comes from neglect of the full spectrum of love in favor of a high-powered microscope placed over the genitals.

It seems to be our younger people who are paying the highest price for this overconcentration on sex, all those beautiful long-haired kids who enjoy calling themselves the Now Generation: "Never mind about yesterday, and we don't want to hear about tomor-row. All true living is in the present. And that's *now*."

That's all very fine, Norman, up to a point. After that, it's just plain foolish. Obviously there's nothing positive about brooding over the past, nor is there much sense to putting everything off till tomorrow. But this growing need for instant gratification carries its own built-in time bomb. And some of our most distinguished sex excavators seem to have taken on the role of Pied Piper in leading this children's crusade to Lollypop Land. Whether they realize it or not, these blessed doctors, these media-oriented sex experts, have actually presented today's kids with a kind of semi-official justification for their dictum of fun and games and a lack of goals. And I believe a lack of real goals is going to be their single biggest cause of problems—not only for them as individuals, but for their closest relationships. Which is exactly where the love factor gets its lumps.

What they seem to suffer from most is a pleasure fixation. They say, "What the hell, let's have it for kicks." And by forgetting about long-term goals, by ignoring all psychological factors and needs, they've evolved into a pack of monsters who continually require something sweet for survival. When two of them are living together and there's some sort of problem to be faced and worked out, the whole relationship explodes. If they have the slightest trouble getting their candy at home, they quickly search elsewhere. And the soaring divorce rate among the twenty-five- to thirty-five-year-olds offers its own grim testimony to that search. They can't cope with love, because in many cases they actually *can't* love; they haven't the *ability* to love. They may have the ability to screw, but that's just where some of the worst confusion lies. Because many of them actually believe screwing is pretty much what love *is*.

As far as knowing what the total range and meaning of that emotion is about, they haven't the foggiest idea. And I know of too many cases in which doctors are busy treating the physical sides of love problems as if they also thought this was all there was to it (as with Victor Kazinski) instead of treating the neuroses and sociological factors that may have been the real causes of the sexual malfunctions—the fears that may have been holding a woman back from giving of herself emotionally and the conditions that may have been making a man feel less of a man.

A woman's inability to give of herself completely, rarely has anything to do with a physical problem. It's usually an emotional blockage that keeps her from letting go sexually. And as far as a man's impotence is concerned, only about three percent of all such cases are due to physical reasons. The trouble with the other ninety-seven percent is strictly in the head.

I was once treating a man named Friedhoff who, after about fifteen years of marriage, suddenly found he couldn't get it up with his wife anymore. There was nothing wrong with the guy physically. He could arouse himself easily enough while fantasizing about other women. But when he tried to perform with his wife, he went instantly dead. Once Friedhoff started telling me about his wife, it was all clear enough. He just couldn't put up with what the woman had become. She had grown sloppy. She had gotten fat. She had let herself go to the point where she was an absolute physical mess. All of which caused an instinctive resentment, an actual physical revulsion in her husband. Where he had once found her attractive, he had grown to dislike her. But he couldn't tell her. He was too kind a man for that. He couldn't bring himself to hurt her feelings, to tell her, "You've let yourself get fat and ugly. You're sloppy. You don't bathe enough. You smell. I can't stand to look at you so how can I want to touch you? How could you do this to yourself, to me, to *both* of us?"

So because he was unable to say these things to her, because his ability to speak was blocked, the only way he could finally say it was with his penis. The thing flatly refused to respond to his demands. It balked. In the total sense, Friedhoff had stopped loving his wife. And if a man doesn't love a woman, yet continues to live with her, their sex must finally die with his desire. Lack of real love, of affection, of a full relationship and everything that goes with it—the absence of these things is eventually going to ruin sex. It may not ruin it at the beginning. The excitement of a new affair can carry things along for awhile. But a man can't live with a woman over a period of years, suffer an absence of love, and expect good sex to continue.

When the initial freshness and stimulation of a physical relationship finally wanes, as it must, there has to be enough warmth, tenderness, and simple affection left to fill the gap. You can't separate love from sex at that stage without harming or destroying both.

As far as Friedhoff was concerned, I'm afraid I had no magical formula with which to solve his problem. His impotence was curable enough—all he needed was a woman other than his fat sloppy wife as a partner. Which I recommended as therapy and to which he was happy to subscribe. But his wife wasn't about to change into a different woman, and because Friedhoff was locked into her father's business, he couldn't leave her without also leaving all financial security. Freud may well consider sex to be our strongest driving force, but when it comes up against money and the insecurities of approaching middle age, I'm afraid it's not even a contest.

This may sound sadly cynical, Norman, but sometimes I'm sure more marriages are held together by money, or the lack of it, than by love.

But not mine—not my marriage, Norman. Neither love nor money were able to hold that one together. Yet strangely, even at the end we did love each other. It was just that we found it impossible to live in the same house. We tore at each other until we were in pieces. A glance, a careless word, could set an army of demons loose. What vanity, what hurt, what hopeless rage. What a goddamn waste. In the midst of love, two enemies slept side by side.

And now? Well, now I haven't even let her know I'm dying.

October 6

When barbara and i were still newlyweds, Norman, I once walked in on her while she was bathing. She was self-conscious about her nakedness, and my opening the bathroom door startled and embarrassed her.

"Hey!" she said. "Isn't a person entitled to any privacy in this marriage?"

"No," I told her. "It's in the contract. No secrets from the husband."

I stared at her in the tub, her body half in, half out of the water. I couldn't look at her in those days without wanting to devour her, and her vulnerability at that moment made her doubly exciting. "Move over," I said. "I'm coming in."

"You're not!" she yelled.

I started taking off my clothes. "Watch me."

"Please," she said. "Please don't. I *mean* it."

I looked at her and saw that she did mean it. I stopped undressing and knelt beside the tub. "What's wrong, darling?"

"Nothing's wrong." She stared at a piece of soap in her hands. "I just don't think I'd like that."

"You've never even tried it," I said. "How do you know?"

"I just know."

"Hey, that's silly."

"So, it's silly," she said. "But it just happens to be the way I feel. Unless it's also in the contract that I can't have feelings different from my husband's."

Still on my knees, I felt stupid and rejected. The whole thing seemed to have gotten out of hand. I was hurt, and the only way I knew to cover my hurt was with anger. So I got up, said something bitter and cutting and stormed out of the bathroom.

It took a while for her to be able to talk about it. I was in bed with my eyes closed, pretending to be asleep, when she asked softly, "Are you sleeping?"

"Yes," I said.

"I'm sorry," she said. "I'd like to explain."

I opened my eyes and waited.

"I had some kind of rash on my backside. It was ugly. I didn't want you to see it."

I turned and looked at her. "That's all?" I asked. "That's the whole thing?"

She nodded.

"Why didn't you tell me?" I said.

"That would have been almost as bad as having you see it."

"But you're telling me now."

"It's better now," she said. "It's gone away."

"You mean I'm never to be allowed to see any-thing about you that's less than absolute perfection?"

"Not if I can prevent it," she said.

"Jesus, you need help."

"So?" she said. "*You're* the shrink. *Help* me."

I kissed and held her. "For God's sake, don't you know how much I love you?"

"I know."

"So, how could you think a goddamn pimple on your ass would make me love you any less?"

"It wasn't a pimple," she said with dignity. "It was a rash."

I said, "Call it what you want; I think we're both in trouble."

And we were, Norman. Because in my own way I was as bad as she. I could show no blemish either, physical or otherwise. In fact I was worse. At least she was able to explain afterward. I never could. And that was probably the worst blemish of all. So, even loving each other as we did, we had our lonely, secret places. And because we were ashamed of them, we kept them locked from each other.

So we wasted a lot. But time did make some things better, Norman. At least it made Barbara less self-conscious about nakedness. Or, if she never truly got over being embarrassed by it, she did manage to handle it better. She even learned to enjoy making love during the day, or with the lights on at night, which was a major victory, considering all she had to overcome. And with her new courage, she found herself intrigued, even fascinated by my body. She would sometimes stare at it.

"What an absolutely amazing thing," she once said.

"What?" I asked.

"That thing of yours."

"That thing of mine has a name," I told her.

"All right," she conceded. "Your *penis*."

I grinned. I enjoyed that part of her shyness. It delighted me. And of course knowing how I felt, she probably played up to it. "That may be anatomically correct," I said, "but it has the ring of a medical text. There are more informal, more friendly names for it."

"They're not friendly to me," she said. "They're obscene."

"Spoken with love," I said pompously, "there's no such thing as an obscenity."

"I love you and I love *it*," she said, "but I don't think I could ever say those names."

"Well, it's no tragedy," I told her.

But later on, Norman, as the movies, the theater, contemporary literature, and our friends became increasingly free in their use of what had once been considered gutter language, she began to feel out of step. "Is there something wrong with me?" she asked. "Everyone but me seems able to use those awful words."

"You're fine," I said. "There's something wrong with *them*."

"I'm serious," she said. "I'm beginning to feel like an anachronism. Maybe I should at least *try*."

"All right. We'll start setting up practice sessions."

I was joking, but she wasn't. She did try. Being conscientious in whatever she did, she was also conscientious about this. She brought it to bed with us, introduced her new language into our love making. At first it took a lot of effort, then less and less until she was able to say the required words quite easily. At times, making love, the things she said even began to excite her. And curiously, coming from that sweet, shy, forever virginal mouth, they began to excite me too.

"How am I doing?" she asked after one of her better efforts.

"Great," I said.

"Am I starting to sound like a whore in bed?"

"I don't know," I told her. "I've never heard a whore in bed."

"What worries me," she said, "is that I think I'm starting to *enjoy* saying all these awful things."

"Don't let it worry you," I said. "The words aren't important."

"What's important?" she asked.

"That you love me. And never stop."

"I do love you," she said, "and you *know* I'll never stop."

That's how we talked then. Close or apart, love held us like cement. Sometimes I'd lay beside her as she slept, satisfied to touch the tip of a finger to some point, *any* point on her flesh. I could almost *feel* things flow between us. When I was happy, touching her made me happier. When I was tired, it freshened me. When I was worried, it lifted me out of it.

Watching her sleep, I'd try to imagine what she was dreaming, what secret events were going on from which I was barred. I felt curiously left out at such moments. With her eyes closed, her face relaxed, her breathing regular, she seemed quite complete without me. She was a consistently sound sleeper, and though I'd sometimes try to waken her by staring, by the force of my will, I never could. She appeared very young as she slept, a soft, pink child, her skin almost luminous, even when she was well past the age for any such look.

But I remember she did once wake to find me staring at her. She blinked as she came up out of sleep. "Hey, what are you looking at?"

"You," I said.

She made a face. "That's unfair. Please don't watch me while I sleep. I must look awful."

"You look beautiful."

"I don't believe you," she said. "I'm sure I snore with my mouth wide open."

"You look seventeen and delicious."

"Honest?"

"I swear."

"Then I'll let you watch me sleep," she said. And damned if she didn't close her eyes, Norman, and go off again within minutes. She had that purity of conscience.

She was an easy sleeper and usually fell asleep first. But once I went off ahead of her and was startled awake as she stirred against me. "What ... what ... what?" I mumbled.

"I'm sorry I woke you," she said. "That was terrible of me."

"What's wrong?"

"Nothing's wrong," she said. "I just hate it when you fall asleep first."

"I don't usually."

"I know," she said. "But you did tonight. And I think I was a little frightened."

"Of what?" I asked.

"I have this crazy feeling you might never wake up."

"I'll wake up," I told her. "I have a very busy day tomorrow."

"Isn't sleeping supposed to be a little like dying?" she asked.

"A little," I said. "Only less permanent."

"Do you think I'm crazy?"

"Yes," I said. "But not enough to have you committed."

"Would you ever commit me?"

"Not unless you kept waking me up," I said.

She sighed. "I hope I die first. I hate the thought of sleeping without you."

"You're a barrel of laughs tonight," I said. "How did we ever get into this?"

"You fell asleep ahead of me."

"I'll never do it again," I promised. And I don't think I ever did.

In those days bed was the center of the universe. It was that important to us. No matter how separate we were during the day, it always brought us together

at night. Without my wife, bed was a lonely landscape. Some of my worst moments have been spent
lying alone in the night, my thoughts leaden with
dread. But never with Barbara beside me. And however bad things got for us later, at night we always
declared an armistice. We would never hurt each
other in bed.

These nights, I miss her terribly.

October 7

A BEAUTIFUL DAY, Norman. Lately I find I've been feeling kind of down on such days, but it hasn't happened yet this morning. So far, I'm feeling okay. I know it will change in an hour or two, but right now I'm accepting it gratefully. Which is a rare thing for me. I've never been very good at accepting the present on its own terms.

I remember you once telling me of the satisfaction you got out of teaching art to beginners because of their excitement and enthusiasm, because of the conscious joy they found in their newly awakened awareness. You said they were learning to see because they were becoming artists, and becoming artists because they were learning to see. A magical two-way process. A fascinating beginning. And one that I imagine must be very like the beginnings of love.

I remember how clear and lovely it always seemed during those first few times together. I used to look into a woman's eyes and feel certain I had found warmth, love, the basic truths of my life—past, present and future. God, what a feeling! Only it never lasted. I'd get to know her, she'd get to know me, and neither of us could live up to the other's dreams. Like most of us, I later learned to temper my dreams. And right there, I guess, is where we first begin to die a little.

Still, it's all a natural enough part of the love cycle, with one part cemented to the others with small patches of pain and disappointment. And not even the patches should be avoided, because the hurt also has its role. It pushes us along. When we try too hard to remain untouched, to avoid that occasional kick in the gut that's part of the whole thing, something even more damaging can result. And part of that something, Norman, I think I'm going to have to lay at the feet of the famous Dr. Alfred Kinsey himself.

Kinsey was, of course, an innovator. It's important to remember that. He was the first to say that sexual behavior in humans *could* be studied, which was surely a unique and beneficial thing at that point in time. At least he asked questions, got answers, and published the results. But Kinsey did *not* study love. He studied sexual behavior—and in the process, helped reduce our love making to the level of animals.

Of course one of the reasons Kinsey emphasized

the physical part of love above all else was because he was an ethologist, one of those involved with the scientific study of animal behavior. In fact his specialty was zoology, which tended to make him animalize humans in his investigations of them. He studied mechanical sex as practiced and enjoyed by animals, and the published results of his studies have often proved calamitous to a lot of people in the much more sensitive and complicated areas of human love. In any case, they did affect a one-time patient of mine named Gary Martin. And what happened to Gary, undoubtedly happened to a lot of others during the post-Kinsey years.

Gary was in his late twenties when he first came to me, a shy, withdrawn young man who worked as an actuary for an insurance company. He had few relationships away from his office; he lived alone and told me he hadn't gone out with a girl in more than five years. I asked him why not. Didn't he like women? Oh, he liked *them* well enough, he said, but they never seemed to care very much about *him*. In fact the last few times he went out, he had found it so painful that he just never bothered to try again.

When it came to the subject of sex, it turned out that he had a normal enough drive but kept the pressure from rising to uncomfortable heights by masturbating. It just wasn't worth it to him to take a girl out, spend a lot of money on her, suffer an evening of painful doubt and rejection, end up feeling utterly miserable, and probably not be able to get her into bed with him anyway. He wasn't much good at conversation, and with the additional tensions of trying to make a good impression, and just plain nervousness, the evenings were pure hell for him. Of *course* he wanted to have a woman, he said. Of *course* he wanted to share his thoughts with her, share hers in return, feel her beside him in the night. Damn it! Wasn't he a man like other men? That's why he was here with me now. To try to help himself to do it.

And what about the past five years I asked. Why hadn't he made even a single attempt? Well, he said, maybe if he hadn't been able to satisfy his sexual needs alone, he might have been forced to try. He might have been forced to learn how to talk properly to a woman, how to be comfortable with her, how to establish some sort of relationship. This much he admitted.

Then came his justifications—his list of quotes from Dr. Kinsey, the zoologist whose manual was his constant bedside companion, his bible. Clearly Onan wasn't alone. *Blessed be those who cast their seed upon the ground, for their number are legion.* I mean, said Gary, look at all the goddamn statistics. Look at all these guys who do it to themselves, and they don't go crazy or blind or get warts on their hands. For God's sake, Dr. Flavin! The book practically says it's healthy. It's even *good* for you. And it certainly beats hell out of letting some broad treat you like dirt and not even put out.

Well, he did know enough, finally, to be aware of th kind of trouble he was in. At least he was able to scrape together enough sense to make him go somewhere other than to Kinsey's bloody manual for help.

All those statistics! Swallow enough and they'll choke the miracle of human love right out of you. So there he was, sitting at home for five long years with his sad little thing in his hand, while untold numbers of equally lonely women, his female counterparts, remained untouched, unspoken to, unloved. Between Kinsey's statistics and Masters and Johnson's vibrators, there sometimes seems to have been a deliberate masturbatory conspiracy by the scientific community to keep men and women from ever finding and enjoying one another in bed.

Don't misunderstand me, Norman. As I mentioned before, Kinsey was an outstanding pioneer in his field and did a fine job of scholarship in compiling his statistics. However, his work did spread a fair amount of confusion among those most vulnerable in that area, among poor lonely souls like Gary Martin, who considered his findings on the subject of masturbation as officially sanctioning it as an acceptable substitute for the real thing. Which it obviously is not.

Or maybe not so obviously. At least not to those men and women who may be shy and without the confidence to build the kind of relationship needed between two people before love can result. Like Gary, a lot of these people were falsely encouraged to rid themselves of the very sexual tension that might otherwise have driven them to seek one another out.

What would happen to them finally is that they would just stop trying. They would stop trying to make themselves appealing. They would stop trying to develop the social skills needed to attract someone they might care about. And they would also stop trying to accept and deal with the inevitable hurt that is, unfortunately, a natural part of the love cycle.

But it wasn't only among the uncertain and the lonely that Kinsey's flood of statistics did its damage. His published figures on all areas of sexual activity, normal and abnormal, single, double, and multiple, created their own unique areas of havoc. The thing was, Norman, that our happily rampant zoologist put out a series of numbers for us which, when broken down, established all sorts of schedules and timetables on human sexual activity. Nailing down everything by age group, educational background, profession, and industry, the doctor presented us with an irrefutable set of guidelines as to what we might consider our high, low, and average activities in the bedroom.

Just picture this for a minute, Norman. Here's this nice, reasonably well adjusted twenty-nine-year-old architect from Tulsa, Oklahoma, named Meaker, who has been happily married for five years. He's the father of two children and is earning twenty-one thousand dollars a year. He loves his wife, enjoys what he feels to be a good and ample sex life with her and, like most of us, considers himself a truly superior lover in both performance and frequency. Until one quiet Sunday afternoon when Meaker casually picks up and glances through Kinsey's Great Book of Sexual Facts and Numbers and suddenly finds himself in a cold sweat.

My God, he thinks, there's something wrong. I'm a sexual failure. I can't let Francine see this. Maybe I'd better get myself examined by a doctor. For the last six weeks I've been way below my norm. I'm not even thirty years old and I can't keep up anymore.

According to the Kinsey timetables he has just read, he should be making love to his wife at least four and a half times a week. And for the past six weeks, he has averaged only one and a half times. If he doesn't start moving things along more quickly, he'll *never* catch up. The fact that during the past six weeks he has been under unusual pressure in the office and has been tired and tense when he arrived home, doesn't make his dismal box score any easier to accept. The figures are all right there, and they say nothing about any of his office problems. All they say is that a married guy in his age group, with his particular family, profession, and educational and sociological background, should be making it with his wife a very specific four and a half times a week if he wants to consider himself of at least average effectiveness sexually.

So whether he feels in the mood or not, Meaker starts rushing a very surprised Francine into action in order to build up his sagging averages. With the result that he's soon loving more and enjoying it less. Instead of erotic visions swimming in his brain, instead of the inspiration of genuine desire, Meaker's passion has been reduced to a neatly organized series of numbers—his moving averages. And you can pretty well imagine what that could do to any hope of a relaxed and spontaneous sex life.

Now, I consider myself pretty sophisticated about this sort of thing. I mean I *know* how subject to interpretation, how much of a lie figures and statistics can be. Plus the fact that many of Kinsey's statistics were additionally faulted in that they left out blacks, Mexican-Americans, Indians, Puerto Ricans, and God knows how many other ethnic groups. Yet I must admit to an occasional furtive glance, over the years, at his goddamn sex tables. Stupid, huh? All right. But how else was I supposed to know whether or not I was keeping up with my age group?

October 8

I'M HAVING MORE TROUBLE than usual sleeping tonight, Norman, so I'm going to help myself get
through it by talking to you. It sure beats just lying
here and thinking. Anyway, a kind of crazy thought
hit me a few minutes ago and I wanted to share it
with you.

One of the small ironies of love (or of the ani-
malistic thing it's being reduced to by the sex excavators), is the fact that there happens to be a piece of
stuff at the base of the male spine that is actually an
erection center. And interestingly, it can be stimulated by even so genderless and unerotic a source as
an electric current. Even if a man is unconscious, an

electrical impulse, properly placed, can create an erection that is quite apart from his knowledge and control.

So as I see it, this could well bring us to the ultimate in the purely mechanical approach to sex towards which many of our doctors seem to be leading us. No emotional involvements, no desire, no passion, no feeling of love, no nothing. Just flick the switch, turn on the juice and you're primed and ready to go.

Let's assume we have a patient with severe emotional problems who is unable to achieve an erection. He has tried everything. He has gone to priests, rabbis, faith healers, and doctors, and his thing is still as dead as Kelsy's. So what happens? We lay him down, attach an electrode to the proper place at the base of his spine, give him a quick jolt, and wham! A living monument to love.

Can you imagine the possibilities? And it's not really that far-fetched. Haven't we already gone even further with our pace-makers? Haven't we already implanted these little wonder gadgets in the chests of thousands of patients to stimulate their failing heartbeats? Why couldn't we also install erection-makers, where necessary, on the same basis? Why should it be considered any more unusual than contact lenses or hearing aids? It's merely an aid of a different sort. It might even be carried externally, although this wouldn't be nearly as feasible as an implant.

What a blessing for the hopelessly impotent of the world! Just imagine this guy, Norman. After months of waiting, of preparation, he finally has his love in bed. Tremblingly, fearing his usual chronic impotence, he presses his new little wonder machine and transforms himself instantly into a roaring stud. And what great commercial possibilities. Doctors have become primarily businessmen with stethoscopes anyway. They could now make even greater fortunes. Their sex clinics could market them as Do-It-Yourself-Erection-Sets, complete with detailed instructions, a year's unconditional guarantee, and rechargeable batteries.

Christ, I'm really running silly now. Forgive me, Norman. This hasn't been one of my better nights.

I remember my father also had trouble sleeping near the end, yet refused to take any sleeping pills. He despised all medication. "When I have to sleep," he'd say, "I'll sleep. Finally, I'll sleep forever. So what's the rush? Don't worry about me." He was always telling me not to worry about him. And he meant it. He was a great believer in the natural course of things. Not that he would ever have considered himself a fatalist. What he felt could be changed, he would try to change. Otherwise, he was smart enough just to shrug and accept it.

I find myself thinking of my father more and more often lately. At this point you try to look for signs of continuity. I guess my father tried it too, although with him it was a try at religion. I call it a try, because I think he attempted it as one last shot in the dark. How could it hurt? He rather hoped that if God was watching over him, He had also watched over his father and grandfather and all ancestors, dead and gone before them, as they moved from life in this world to life in some other place. It helped break down the loneliness for him. At least I hope it did. He never revealed very much to me about such things. He was a little suspicious of me after I became a psychiatrist—as if I could no longer be trusted to respond purely from love and might be sitting in judgment.

My father was proud of my becoming a doctor, but disappointed that I wasn't a *doctor* doctor, a *real* doctor who eased *real* pain and cured *real* sickness. Psychiatry confused him. It dealt with the *meshuganas*, the crazies, and those who just thought they were *meshuganas*. He believed there wasn't much to be done for such people anyway, except maybe to love them. And you didn't have to spend all those years studying to be a doctor to do that. Besides, how could you *pay* somebody to love you? It has taken me a long time to discover it, but my father was not entirely wrong.

Although he never finished high school, my father knew as much about the subject of love as anyone I've ever known. At the age of fifteen he took my mother's hand and didn't let go until she died. Love was his familiar. He lived with it on a daily basis. He not only carried it in his heart, he carried it in his stomach along with his digestive juices. So far as I know, he never loved any woman other than my mother, and she never loved any man but him. I don't know what sort of sex life they shared, because such things were neither mentioned nor discussed. But I never even thought of my parents that way. Mom was just mom, dad was just dad, they were there to love you and for you to love, and that was pretty much the whole thing. And if my father had any advice at all to offer on life, living, and human relations, it was, "Don't be alone. There's nothing worse in this world. One person alone is nothing. With just one other, everything changes."

And he was right about that too.

So, naturally I'm ending up alone.

Everyone lives in their own magic landscape, Norman. My father's was decorated by the belief that people were people and that if you gave them half a chance, they'd turn out all right. And this from a man who arrived here an infant out of the pogroms of Russia, who grew up being called *sheeny*, *kike*, and *Jew bastard*, and who lived most of his days blind in one eye because a bunch of tough Irishers thought two eyes might give a Jew too much of an advantage.

I have my own secret land, but it's crude and graceless compared with my father's. There were those who called my father stupid, who said he didn't even have sense enough to know when crap was being thrown in his face, but he was a lot smarter than any of them. He refused to waste time or energy on useless anger. And to him, bitterness was worst of all. What for? All you did was eat out your own *kishkes*. Ulcers and colitis he didn't need. And *this*, without even a medical degree.

But he could be bull-headed too, and he was most unyielding about my divorce. It was incomprehensible to him. He absolutely refused to accept the need for it. What kind of *goyish* gentile nonsense was this? A Jew met a woman, loved her, married her, and stayed married to her until she or he was buried. So you *weren't* always happy together. Who was always happy? What's so much with the happy these days anyway? Where did it say in the contract you always had to laugh and sing? What you had to do, mostly, was love.

"Do you still love her?" he asked.

"Yes," I told him.

"Does she still love you?"

I nodded.

"So what's all this craziness?"

I tried explaining. It wasn't craziness. Barbara and I were rending each other, tearing each other apart. We loved, but also hated. We pulled in opposite directions. We threw spears, jabbed with invisible pitchforks. The children felt it and suffered. We took refuge in rages and petty revenges that left us limp and ashamed. She didn't understand my work. She interfered with it. Everything about it seemed to irritate her. And this, in turn, infuriated *me*. Also, I couldn't abide her taste in people or her judgments about them or her values. I found them empty, lacking in depth. She in turn considered me superior, judgmental, abusive, and chauvinistic.

My father listened to my explanations. He sat like a rock, dark eyes flat. When I finished, he looked at me. "*This* is what they took so long to teach you in school? *This* is what makes you such a big professor people should come pay for advice? Well let me tell you something, Mister Doctor Professor. I might not be so smart as you. I might not know so many high-class words. But I know love is love, a marriage is a marriage, children are children, and all the rest is *bubkes*. Nothing!"

I shrugged him off. I was in no mood for all that

simplistic, homespun jazz. But right now, lying where I am in the night, I don't feel nearly so superior.

My father knew what many of us have never quite managed to learn. He knew there was no reasonable exit from love. He knew there was no escape through attitudes, ideology, or logic. The only way out was to stop loving. Deny a love that's still there and alive, and you deny yourself. And even worse, you sentence yourself to a cold and terrible detachment, to emptiness and running. Without being able to say these things, my father knew them. He also knew love's greatest gift was wholeness, and that those who complained of a loss of freedom were just making sounds. Because the only thing love was ever likely to make you lose was the ache of being alone.

I can touch my father through his love, and his father too, and his father before him. I might have once described this feeling as a sense of generation, but now I'm satisfied to call it love. My father and these others lived at different times and in different places, but love and marriage remained the same for them all. The only one it seems to have changed for is me. I might try to justify this. I might try to point out that life is more complicated today than ever before, that what may once have been fairly simple is no longer so. I might also try to bring up such things as the sensitive and demanding nature of my work, the pressures involved, the need to be single-purposed and free of distraction. I might bring up any number of reasons why marriage failed for me and not for them. But what would be the use? It would change nothing.

October 9

WHEN I WAS A SENIOR IN COLLEGE, Norman, I spent
the summer as a camp counselor in the Adirondacks
and met a girl from Bryn Mawr who read Stendahl
and Kierkegaard and seemed to take great delight in
using the word "fuck." Her name was Emily.

Emily was a new experience for me. I had lived for
almost twenty-two years and never known a girl
quite like her. When she gazed at me through her
thick lashes, I felt uncomfortably young behind my
precious veil of sophistication. When she sat on my
lap and laughed at my jokes, I felt as witty as George
Bernard Shaw. And when she let me make love to her
one night in the meadow behind the camp parking

lot, with Tchaikovsky's music coming from some-body's car radio, I felt crushed and subdued by that special wilderness of feeling which the act of love invariably aroused in me.

And then she said, "Did you enjoy fucking me?"

There was a strange hot wind above us, and below the moving tufts of grass, a refreshing coolness. I didn't say anything. I couldn't—after such a filthy blasphemy. That's how strongly I felt about it.

I got over it and forgave her, of course. At the age of twenty-two, my romantic sensibilities were no match for my lust. Anyway, I told myself, it was just a word. Which was true enough technically, but a lie nevertheless. Because it *wasn't* just a word, at least, not to me. It was an ugly, two-backed, horned beast that had come charging into my lovely garden of earthly delights and crapped all over the flowers.

Emily happened to have been at least ten or fifteen years ahead of her time. Young men no longer shock that easily. And although the doctrine of universal love hasn't yet been able to take over the earth, that particular four letter obscenity for the *act* of love does seem to have managed it. It's now everywhere. There's no escaping its sight or sound. In an amazingly short span of time, both its use and respectability have skyrocketed. From the foulest of gutter epithets, from a dirty scrawl on fences and latrine walls, it has been accepted into drawing rooms, places of higher learning, and the finest literature. And who bears much of the responsibility for this beatification of the obscene? You guessed it: *we* do. The doctors.

Again, it was done with the best of motives. Psy-

chologists agreed that people were generally too uptight about certain words and attitudes in regard to
things sexual. It tied them into emotional knots. They
had created their own verbal taboos, and any taboo
must be regarded as restrictive and unhealthy. Bad,
very bad. All that silliness about washing out a child's
mouth with soap because he had said a dirty word,
when everyone with sense knew there was no such
thing as a dirty word, only wrong attitudes. And the
worst of all attitudes was obviously the acceptance of
any sort of inhibition—whether it be verbal, physical, or psychological. Which was reasonable enough.
But only up to a point. There's always that *point*,
Norman. In any liberating swing, there's always the
danger of the pendulum swinging over too far in the
opposite direction. That's exactly what's happened
here. We've overshot our mark and have ended up
somewhere in the pornographic Land of Oz.

So what's the result? What have we got now?
Well what we have is a wholly new strain of insanity
in which the use of the word "fuck" has, in some in-
stances, actually become mandatory. Now, according
to many of the latest love manuals, couples are better
off psychologically if they can refer to sexual intercourse as "fucking," rather than as "making love."
And it's not only the manuals that preach this new
gospel. It's the therapists as well—many of whom are
insisting that the use of the *Word* is almost a moral
duty for their patients if they expect their love lives
to be honest, complete, and natural.

Since part of a generation has already come of age
under this new set of rules, we're beginning to see

some of its results. And from every possible point of view, they strike me as pretty awful. I'm for freedom of expression as much as anyone, but this new dictum has simply gone haywire. Instead of talking about making love, too many of today's kids are talking about fucking or having sex. And this in itself is destructive to the tenderness, warmth, and mystique that should be part of the act of love. It also hurts the survival chances for any lasting relationship. Because to "fuck" is to reduce the whole thing to the animal level.

This new word-disease has even infected some of our more prestigious psychotherapeutic training centers, in which the professors have made it part of the curriculum to teach the use of the Word in the treatment of certain patients. The idea being that if you've got someone with a love problem in a therapy session, you should make them use the Word whenever they refer to sexual intercourse. It may make the patient shudder but will also prove liberating. The professors claim that if the patient has trouble using the Word, he is probably hiding some sort of neurosis. If he tries to give the act of physical love a more poetic or sensitive designation, if he said, "Let's make love, darling," instead of, "Let's fuck, darling," then that means the poor guy is probably repressed and inhibited and must learn to let go.

So as the end product of all this emphasis on liberation, what we finally get are some of the tough, wildly liberated young people I've had passing through my office over the past few years. These are the kids to whom the Word has come to represent all of love, the ones who make the big singles scenes in our urban centers, who nightly hang out at the bars and discos, who go to these places in the same way one might go to a meat market to select the main course for that night's dinner.

For a while all this activity may seem exciting and stimulating, but then it just becomes pathetic. I've had cases, both male and female, who have found they must finally get high on pot, pills, or alcohol even to function under such conditions. With so much fucking and so little love making, this is what they're ultimately driven to.

If we want to look at it coldly, Norman, we can't actually take too much sexual freedom. How far to the other extreme can we let ourselves be carried by St. Sigmund's revolution? Because what it comes down to is that total sexual license, without moral and sociological guidelines to hold it in check, is not even human. It diminishes us. It leads directly to the degradation of sex on impulse, of indulging ourselves without modesty or discrimination, of walking along somewhere, seeing an appealing piece of flesh of the opposite sex, and going at it like dogs in the street.

We haven't yet quite pushed it there, but how far off are we when some young man can walk into a different bar each night, survey the room, think— hey, there's a cute chick at that table—sit down with her, go through a few moments of the standard obligatory dialogue of . . . "Hey . . . like wow! You know . . . I mean, crazy like . . . I'm into this groovy scene . . ." For Christ's sake, Norman! Some of these brainchildren have three degrees and can't even speak

English anymore. Anyway, the guy goes through some syncopated prattling, maybe has another drink or two with the girl, invites her back to his pad, and in a few minutes, bang! They're in bed doing the Word.

Maybe that's not actually jumping the girl in the street, but how far removed is it? And much of the responsibility for this, along with many of our young people's other problems, lies with those experts who espouse the total joy and freedom of sex without inhibiting factors, performed along strictly natural lines.

It has become so natural it's almost like going to the bathroom. And it's to this that they've pretty much managed to reduce the act of love. They claim that since sex is a natural bodily function, it should be enacted without inhibition. Well, that's fine, Norman. Except that in the process of achieving all this naturalness, they've also managed to remove any of the lovely mystique that may have once belonged to the act, any of the wilderness of feeling through which I had once blundered on some moving tufts of grass to the music of Tchaikovsky, before Emily herself had ruined it.

October 10

I HAVE REALLY COME TO look forward to these taping sessions, Norman. They have obviously become a refuge for me. I think I'm also getting better at them, less self-conscious and more honest. Though it's not easy to judge your own candor, to monitor your prejudices and more subtle motivations.

Right now I'm wondering about my honesty in attacking those young people and their easy sex. Who knows? Maybe part of it was just jealousy. Which can't be ruled out, you know. Because I *am* jealous, Norman, jealous for when I was young, *their* age, and had none of that casual love available. My God, when I think of how I had to struggle, how I had to plan and maneuver just to touch a girl, when I think of all that effort, all those fruitless campaigns. And now all these lucky kids have to do is reach out and pluck the grapes from the vine.

Or maybe not so lucky?

Because I also remember all they're *not* going to have—all that wishing and dreaming and wondrously awkward groping, all those gentle promises and wisps of burning joy. Even the failures, with their misty sadness, carried their own rewards.

So maybe not so lucky.

And that's not just sour grapes, Norman. I really wouldn't trade any of that part with them. Nor would I make any deals for most of the rest. Maybe it didn't seem like so much at the time, but what did I know about it then? *Now* I know what it meant to wake up beside a sleeping face I loved, to watch it in the soft dawn light and know, when it woke, I'd see love in return. And what sweet mysteries that sleeping face did hold. Because I didn't really know anything about girls. It might have been different if I'd had sisters, but I didn't. So those first girls might as well have come to me from some secret place beyond the Himalayas or an Italian nunnery. While I was out playing baseball and stickball and Johnny-Ride-the-Pony, what were they doing? Sewing little dolls' clothes and jumping rope? If there's an overall plan to everything, they must have been preparing for me then, preparing for those unseen moments of love to come.

Christ, how little I knew! My father told me nothing. Just as his father had told *him* nothing. If my father thought of it at all, I'm sure it was with the belief that such things took care of themselves in time. Though he did mention it once when I was about fifteen. "I guess you know about girls," he said. "Just be careful. Don't get in trouble. A little fun for a few minutes can give you a lot to worry about for a long time."

Even that held more warning than information. It assumed I knew what the fun was all about. Which I did. But only up to a point. For one thing, I knew how *I* felt, how certain movements, touchings, embraces affected *me*, affected my body and emotions. But I had no knowledge whatsoever of what my partner might be experiencing, how *she* might be feeling. I guessed she must be feeling pretty good also. But precisely how and what she felt? Well, that was probably the greatest mystery of all.

My first brief glimpse behind that particular wall was offered on the mohair living-room couch of a girl whose name I no longer remember. We were doing what was then called heavy petting, which meant everything but the "real thing." The real thing was called "going all the way." And the most pertinent piece of information you could learn about a girl was the answer to the question, "Does she go all the way?" A question which, incidentally, always infuriated me when asked by one or another of my friends who wanted to know how I had made out the night before.

Didn't the fools know there was no such thing as a girl who went all the way indiscriminately unless she were a nymphomaniac or a whore? And if my date of the night before had, by some sweet miracle, granted me full passage to the Holy Land, why couldn't my silly friends realize it was only because it was *me*, Robert Flavin. And that this didn't mean she'd go all the way with the likes of *them*. It was me, me, me! No one else but *me*! And that was the best part of it all, that lovely afterglow which said that this desirable female person had trusted me enough, had judged me unique and special enough to be granted her most precious gift. The act itself may have been awkward, fumbling, and over very quickly, but who cared? Look at all I had to carry away with me afterward.

Anyway, Norman, to get back to my petting on the mohair couch and my first glimpse into that greatest mystery of them all, the female orgasm.

Of course I didn't know it by that name then. In fact I didn't know it by *any* name. All I knew was that in the midst of our clutching and touching and heavy breathing, the girl suddenly went into a sort of spasm, bit my ear almost clear through, gasped of her love in a choking voice, and then went limp in my arms. Wow, I thought. I was awed. Was I really the cause of all this? Evidently. How marvelous. What a superb lover I must be. How this girl loves me. Now I must make it happen again.

But when I tried to repeat, doing all the same things I had done before, nothing happened. In fact after a short while, the girl (whose name I somehow still don't remember) seemed to have had enough of me and just wanted me to go home. I was no longer awed. My ear was bleeding like a stuck pig's and I was shattered. I didn't understand. How could she be in an absolute frenzy about me one moment, and bored and indifferent the next? What had I done wrong? What kind of girl was she? What kind of lover was *I*?

Confused and hurt, I found no answers to my questions that night. I can find no conclusive answers even now to the enigma of the female orgasm. But then neither can the females themselves, nor the myriads of doctors and professors who have come to specialize in the probing of that particular mystery. They may claim to have the answers, but they don't. All they have is a growing list of theories and an increasingly obsessive need to further its deification. Until it has finally come to be worshipped by all involved, by participants and spectators alike, as nothing less than the Great God Orgasm.

Among large numbers of our new breed of sexual sophisticate, it's no longer enough for a woman merely to enjoy an average run-of-the-mill climax. Hell, no! Not after listening to some of our scientific preachers on salvation-through-orgasm. And certainly not after reading the latest set of inspirational manuals on How to Climax and Find God. Today, if one of these orgasm worshippers doesn't go off like Vesuvius, if she doesn't literally feel the earth move, she thinks she's being cheated.

I've heard them moan, Norman. "Doctor, there must be something seriously wrong with me. I'm told, I've heard, and I've read in books that I'm missing a great deal. Maybe I just can't let go past a certain point. . . ." Or even worse, they blame it on their partners and create an entirely new set of problems. Can you imagine all that pressure building up? It's like expecting a tennis player to serve only aces or else forfeit the match. So naturally the guy is in trouble before he even takes off his shoes.

He tries. He does his best. And in most cases that should be pretty good. After all, he *is* in decent enough physical shape, and he *has* been around awhile. He knows the score. But with his woman setting such high goals, he needs a little encouragement from her. He needs to be told how well he's doing. So he keeps pestering her. "How's it going, honey? Is it great for you? Come on, baby ... come on, darling! Is it lovely? Is it the greatest? Is it the absolute end, sweetheart? Tell me ... tell me ... tell me! ..."

If he doesn't, God forbid, make the earth move for her, he has to consider it now *his* failing, *his* inadequacy. Why? Because he has also read the sex bibles. He has also listened to the evangelists of the orgasm and knows what's expected of him.

But with all this knowledge, he doesn't realize that what his partner wants least at this moment is his prattling about how things may be going for her. What she *does* want and need from him is some plain old spontaneity, just his letting himself go. *This* is what she would find exciting at her moment of climax. *This* is what would have the greatest chance of launching her into space.

How sadly ironic the whole thing finally becomes, Norman. By the very fact of wanting something so desperately, of working at it so hard, all they manage to do is lose it. If they could only forget the love manuals, forget the advice of the experts, forget the grading of technique, of performance and response— if they could only relax and enjoy the pure intimacy of such a moment, its warmth, closeness and sharing, they could have it all.

In the meantime, the physical and psychological destruction being engendered often borders on the unbelievable. Just listen to this one, Norman. It involves another case of impotence, but this one very different. Because Olsen managed to achieve his condition in a unique way.

Originally, Olsen's problem was that he judged himself a victim of premature ejaculation. I say judged, because it was by his own time estimate that he diagnosed his case—about twenty minutes. When he lost control and climaxed after this long a period of steady love making, he considered his climax premature. Twenty minutes simply wasn't good enough; certainly not after he had read in some of the love manuals that really good studs would be able to keep things going for at least two or three hours. Why some sex clinics even preached that such extended periods of joy were to be considered the sexual order of the day. So here he was, going off after only twenty meagre minutes and suffering all sorts of inadequacy feelings.

Olsen finally consulted a doctor about his alleged problem. And what did the doctor do? He prescribed a special salve and told him that if he applied it to his penis during intercourse, it would help control his excitement and keep him from achieving orgasm for a greatly extended period. And how would the salve perform this magic? Simply by anesthetizing the penis, literally putting it to sleep while erect.

You find it hard to conceive of a physician doing this? The world, Norman, is populated by an incredible number of horse's asses, and here we have two of the biggest, who have somehow managed to find one another. A trained medical professional who would actually prescribe so idiotic a treatment, and an otherwise intelligent adult, a successful electronics engineer, who would voluntarily submit to it. Because what this alleged remedy was going to do was desensitize the penis to a point where all the excitement, all the pleasure, all the traditionally expected bliss of the act of love was totally removed.

But Olsen went along with it, and as far as he was concerned, it did what the doctor had promised it would do. It allowed him to make love for much longer periods of time. The man was so mixed up in his thinking that he was willing to sacrifice most of his own sexual pleasure, was willing to dull his senses to the point where he felt almost *nothing*, to turn out a more impressive technical performance.

Until it came time for the Devil to collect. An invisible system of checks and balances, Norman, in one way or another usually evens things out. Anyway, Olsen at last reached the point where the suspending of the pleasure factor began also to suspend his ability to achieve an erection. In fact it put that miraculous ability to sleep entirely and with apparent permanence, leaving him with a real, honest-to-God case of impotence. Now he couldn't make love at *all*. And this was the way he came to me as a patient.

It took a long time, but I was eventually able to get him straightened out, by repairing some of the psychological damage done by the love bibles and that idiot doctor. Olsen had been subjugated not only sexually, but in every other way as well. He had lost all confidence, had become withdrawn socially, and wasn't even performing up to par in his work. What that doctor had done was take a perfectly healthy young man and turn him into a psychological wreck by treating a nonexistent ailment. And the damn quack is still in practice, is a revered member in good standing of the medical profession, and is probably getting richer by the day.

Just a brief postscript, Norman, on this whole ridiculous business of sustaining intercourse for longer and longer periods. Some of our more competitive studs seem to be heading for the time when any climax reached in less than three hours is going to be considered premature. And a lot of doctors, who should know better, are going along with this whole distorted view of what the act of love is all about. To the point where they are coming up with all sorts of sparkling ideas to help keep their patients-at-stud hanging in there as long as possible. One of the most frequently offered suggestions I've heard, deals with the "squeeze" technique, in which the stud's partner is urged to apply strong, even violent pressure to his penis just below the head. The theory is that if sufficient pain is caused, the joy of the moment is going to be ruptured enough to let him continue a while longer.

What this may eventually lead to is some as yet unenvisioned peak of sado-masochistic absurdity in which doctors will prescribe more and more pain in order to curb greater and greater amounts of pleasure.

October 11

MOST OF US SEEM TO HAVE an innate need to talk about our loves, Norman. Or our *love*, if there happens to have been only one. It's as though just the act of putting the experience into words, of sharing it, is in itself a needed affirmation. And I suppose it is. Talking nails it down. It lets at least one other person know that we have loved and been loved, and that regardless of the many indictments the world makes, we still retain some fragment of this sweet memory at our core and hold it dear.

I guess we feel that to have loved and been loved can't help but make us appear more lovable. I've sat for years in my office and in other places and listened to them all—the old, the young, the middle-aged, the hard cases and the soft, the lewd and the pious, the amoral and the righteous. I've listened to gangsters, murderers, rapists, the sane and the insane, the rich and the poor, the brilliant and the foolish. And their single common denominator, the one thing they invariably shared, was a compulsive need to let me know how beautifully and completely they had loved.

Look at me is what they're shouting. Pay attention! Never mind how I look. Never mind what I've done. Never mind what anyone says about me. I feel, I care, and I've been cared about.

Then more softly, the eyes say, "Listen. Please love me. We're all of us dying."

Of course, that includes me. Because obviously I'm no special case, no different. And it's clearly to you, Norman, that I've chosen to do my own talking as I make my own final plea for lovability. So let me tell you about the first time I knew adult love and went "all the way" with a girl. I promise to be as objective as possible.

I was eighteen years and four months old at the time. I remember my age so specifically, because I was watching it very carefully during this period. With each passing day, I was wondering more and more desperately how old I was going to be before it finally happened. Sometimes, I despaired. Sometimes, I would wake in the night with this terrible fear of dying a virgin, unknowing, the victim of some nameless but swiftly fatal disease. I began guarding my health like the worst of hypochondriacs. To die so young would be bad enough, but to die without experiencing love's crowning joy was unthinkable, an abomination. I wanted to weep at just the thought. I was also becoming ashamed. Every other guy I knew seemed to have already done it. At least that was what they said. Not that I cared so much about their opinion of me. They didn't know of my untouched state. I always managed a cool, enigmatic silence whenever the subject came up. It was my own opinion I cared about. I was beginning to lose my self-respect.

Then I met Angela. The name, she told me, meant angel. My God! She was older, almost nineteen, and a *shiksa* besides. Both definitely plus factors. She had pale eyes, green as sea water, and beautiful hands with long, delicate fingers. Her hands fascinated me. I kept imagining them doing obscene things. When they accidently touched me—it didn't matter where—I shivered. Around Angela, I was one big erogenous zone.

She wore rustling dresses and cologne, and we talked about art, music, and Life. Sometimes, in the summer sun, she let me rub tanning lotion on her back, her arms, and legs. God, what skin! What Jewish girl had skin like that? It came from five thousand years of white bread and oysters. So naturally I fell madly in love with her. And for some incredible reason—to this day I haven't been able to quite figure out why—she fell madly in love with *me*.

We did everything but go "all the way" and it was beautiful. It was so beautiful I was afraid to spoil it by pressing for more, by going all out for the "real thing." I loved her too much. How could I even *want* to go all the way with someone I loved? That was precisely the kind of convoluted thinking I was heir to in those days. If you were a nice Jewish boy— and what other kind of Jewish boy was there?—you tried to make love only with girls you *didn't* care about, girls you *didn't* love.

But Angela, bless her little golden *shiksa* head, had no such crippling hangups. Her reasoning was less insane than mine. Since we loved one another, since she was sure there would never be anyone whom she could possibly love more than she loved me, what was she saving it for?

And Jews call *shiksas* dumb.

So there we were on a particular night in August, in the walled garden behind Angela's house. Her parents were away and we had dinner outside, by candle-light, under a graceful old elm. We hardly spoke as we ate. When we finished, Angela blew out the candles and we went and sat on a wide, sofa-like glider with a canopy. We sat side by side for a long time, looking up at the stars through the elm. In the hazy light, the surrounding houses faded away and we might have been in a walled garden somewhere in Tibet.

Angela said, "I love you . . . It's all right . . . I want to."

I said, "I love you too. But are you sure? Aren't you afraid?"

Angela said, "I'm afraid, but I'm sure."

She had that much more sense and courage than me.

Since it was the first time for both of us, it must have been fumbling and far from perfect. But if it was, I don't remember it that way. All I remember is thinking afterward, it's all right, God. If you want me to die now, it's perfectly all right.

So Angela loved me. And she loved me enough to have given me this priceless gift. You see, I still thought of the act of love as something a girl *gave*. Angela's pleasure, I felt, came mostly from giving pleasure to *me*. And because I wanted to show her I understood what she had done, because I wanted to give her something of equal value in return, I offered her my life. It was all I had. I asked her to marry me.

Of course this is the stuff of light comedy today, Norman. Here's this silly, starry-eyed kid who makes it with a broad for the first time and thinks he has invented it. Not only that, he's prepared to turn his whole life upside down out of sheer gratitude. Today we know better than to take things so seriously. We expect our eighteen- and nineteen-year-olds to have been hopping in and out of the sack like jack rabbits by that age, to have tried at least half a dozen different partners, and to have been sensible enough to keep it all on a purely physical level. No emotional entanglements.

But back then I didn't have the benefits of all that wisdom and sophistication. All I had was a love that touched and stayed with me from the moment I opened my eyes in the morning until I reluctantly slept at night. All I really wanted from the future was not money, not success, not power or fame—just Angela's love. She was my someone that everyone hopes to have, finally. She was my meaning of life.

Everything I had ever done, from the moment of my birth, seemed to lead me only as far as Angela.

Don't think my offer was made lightly, Norman. I didn't just ask Angela to marry me in the beatific afterglow of passion and then promptly forget about it. I wasn't that kind of eighteen-year-old. I was a pre-sexual-revolution eighteen-year-old. What I said I would do, I intended to do. So naturally I had to tell my father.

When I told him, he just looked at me. My father had great control. Also, he loved and respected me. Regardless of what he felt or thought, he would never be abusive.

"So tell me about her," he said.

My throat dry and constricted, I told him.

"A *shiksa?*"

I tried for a certain dignity. "Her parents are Presbyterian. She's an agnostic."

My father frowned. "So she's *not* a *shiksa?*"

"She's a *shiksa*," I sighed.

"And you love her?"

I couldn't answer that one. I had a terrible fear that if I so much as tried to describe what I felt for this girl, I'd start crying like a baby. So I just nodded.

"When?" he asked.

I stared at my father's right earlobe. In shape and size, it was exactly like mine. Or rather, mine was exactly like his. He liked to joke about it. "See?" he'd say, plucking at my ear, "Exactly like mine. That's how I know for sure you're my son."

"When do you want to get married?" he asked.

I hadn't thought it through that far. I was just about to start my freshman year at college. I wanted to appear as reasonable and mature as possible, so I said, "When I graduate from college." I hadn't yet decided I was going to be a doctor.

"Sensible. An education is important. Without it, you're a cripple in the world."

I waited. This couldn't be all. It was too easy.

"Congratulations," my father said. "I wish you luck. Invite your *shiksela* for dinner Friday night. Momma and I should meet the girl our son is going to marry."

And that was it. My father was smart. He was not about to martyr me with any of the standard objections. That would only push me into doing something precipitous and stupid. Since I had allowed him four years grace, he intended to ride it out. With all that time and the vagaries of youth on his side, how could he lose? I knew how he was thinking, but it was fine with me. Because I knew better. I knew that four years or forty weren't going to make any difference in the way I felt about Angela. I would love her until I died.

And I have, Norman. Or anyway, almost, since I'm not yet quite dead. Maybe my father would have been proved right. Maybe time, youth, and background would really have beaten us. But at least they didn't come anywhere near it for almost a year. Which was just about all the time we had before her older brother flew off with her one spring day in a rented Cessna and never brought her back.

There were storms in the area and they couldn't

find the plane for about thirty-six hours. I was with them when they did find it. They tried to keep me from going, but who was about to stop me?

It didn't look like too bad a wreck when we got there. The plane was mostly in one piece and there hadn't been any explosion or fire. I was very grateful for that part. Idiotic, wasn't it? As if that made any difference. But somehow it did. Because all I kept thinking about were her hands and that incredible skin. And they really looked fine, untouched. So that looking at her, you would have found it hard to tell there was anything wrong.

My father was wonderful. Without ever having taken a course, he did and said all the right things. Not that he could resolve my quarrel with death. Nor can any of us. But at least he knew enough to be there, and to let me weep, and even to say *Kaddish* and mourn for my green-eyed *shiksa* right along with me.

So, that was my Angela.

We had all the ingredients of the classic, star-crossed romantic tragedy—youth, a conflict of religion, intensity of feeling, and devotion to the end. But most especially, we had the dramatic parting while love was at its height. There was no time for it to fade, no chance for it to smash against the practicalities of daily living—against the bills, the problems with the children, the petty squabbling, all the minutiae that can finally do more damage to love than the most cataclysmic events.

Which is undoubtedly why the most famous love

affairs of literature—Romeo and Juliet, Tristan and Isolde, Lancelot and Guinevere—always ended with a tragic drama. Imagine Romeo and Juliet, instead of dying so magnificently, getting married, having six kids, quarreling with each other and their deadly, ever-present relatives, growing fat and veined and red-faced until they finally can't stand the sight of one another. Some quotable cynic once said there were more beautiful love affairs ruined by marriage than by anything else, and the guy may just have been a little bit right.

So I don't know what might have happened if Angela had lived and we had married. Maybe our marriage would have turned out no better than the one I shared with Barbara. I like to think it might have, but of course I'll never know.

Please understand something about my *shiksa*, Norman. She was a good girl. I mean good in the old-fashioned moral sense. Academically, she did not believe in sex out of wedlock. And the only reason she went all the way with me, was because she had fallen totally in love and wanted to offer *everything*, which doesn't mean she ever did it easily or considered it lightly. She went through some heavy soul searching before that night in the garden. Her background and upbringing were morally strict. Her parents were real church-going bluestockings. And even afterward, even after that first time, it didn't get any easier for her. Her only justification for what she still considered a basically immoral act was that she loved me. And because I knew all this, because I knew the importance to her of what she was offering, its value to me was that much greater. It kept me from ever taking either Angela or her love casually.

Not that Angela was especially unique in the way she felt about these things. For the "good" girls of that period, it was a fairly standard approach. When you gave up that particular part of your purity in those days, it had to be for a very good reason. Otherwise, you felt like a tramp. And there were times, even with such allegedly good reasons as deep love and total commitment, when you still felt you had fallen from grace.

There's a totally different kind of thinking around today, Norman, almost a reverse sexual bigotry. Instead of having to fight the guilt of going all the way, today's women have been so thoroughly brainwashed by the Joy Boys and their love manuals that if they don't "express themselves fully" in the sack, it's practically *immoral.*

I've had female patients almost crawl into my office because of the weight of these new ton-loads of guilt they'd been carrying. "I must be sick, doctor," they've told me. "I must be emotionally and sexually repressed." And why did they think they were sick? Because they hadn't allowed themselves to go to bed with men they may have been dating with some regularity, but whom they didn't feel they loved.

So the sex excavators have reversed the old-time guilt and turned it inward. Love and passion are no longer considered the prerequisites for a man and woman going to bed together. As a matter of fact, many psychological counselors are now preaching the exact opposite. They claim too great an emotional in-

volvement can actually damage an otherwise satisfactory physical relationship. How? By putting the
pressure of love's hot little fingers on the pleasantly
uninvolved "coolness" of one or the other of the partners. A total reversal. We once tried to enjoy love
without giving in to the temptation of going all the
way. Now they're trying to enjoy going all the way
without giving in to any true feeling of love.

Maybe you can make some sense of it, Norman. I
can't. For myself, given the choice, I'd still reach
happily for what Angela and I had, still be grateful
for another chance at the uncertainty and soul searching, the commitment without compromise, the love
without temperance. Altogether, we had less than a
year, and it was a long time ago, but it has always
seemed like so much more.

Once, not long after our night in the garden, I saw
her by chance on a Sunday morning. She was on her
way to church with her parents and I watched her
walking with them. I still remember what she was
wearing. She had on a wide straw hat with a bright
red band, and the light thrown on her face was soft
and warm. Her dress was a pale pink and clung as
she walked, showing her hips and breasts. And I remember smiling to myself from the car in which I
was sitting, and thinking, my God, my God, and for
the rest of the day finding it utterly impossible to stop
grinning.

October 12

I BELIEVE I TOLD YOU EARLIER, Norman, that I haven't let my wife—I mean my *former* wife—know I was phasing out. Which means my children don't know either, nor do others who were once close to me. Those few who do know, those involved medically, or whom I had to tell for one reason or another, have promised to honor my wish for privacy in this. Someone may yet decide to tell Barbara anyway. And there are times, Norman, when I think I almost wish they would.

It's a temptation. We're all of us such congenital hams. We plot, anticipate, and cherish most those scenes in which we can play a major part. And what greater, more poignant scene have we got than our final one? So sometimes I let myself fantasize about my own last moments, with Barbara and the kids there, weeping, telling me of their love, of their need for me, of the darkness that will cloud their lives when I am gone. And I—with the easy gentleness of one who had made peace with himself—quietly comfort them, gazing upon them with love, and whisper the parting words they'll remember gratefully for the rest of their days.

Lovely. Except that it doesn't work that way.

We simply don't die like Mimi in *Bohème*, with our voices soaring sweetly to the second balcony. Nor do our loved ones usually weep and speak of their love. What they are, mostly, is anxious, ill at ease, and wondering how much longer the whole unpleasant business is going to take. A lot of appointments have been broken, their daily routines turned into a shambles, and they're already trying to figure out how much more the coming funeral arrangements are going to mess things up. And as far as the dear departing one is concerned, he rarely knows what's going on anyway. He has either been in a coma for several hours or days, or else is so doped up that he's off somewhere on cloud nine, dreaming of his childhood. Before that, when he *was* reasonably aware, he probably just resented the hell out of every erect, ambulatory sonofabitch who was arrogant and insensitive enough to enter his death room and parade his goddamn health and capacity for life up and down in front of him.

So you see, Norman, I don't really want any of

that. If I didn't know it before my mother died, it was something she helped me understand afterward. My mother loved me about as much as it is possible for a mother to love a son, yet her last words to me were, "Why did you put me in this place?" *This place* was the hospital in which she would die shortly of a few assorted technical factors, but mostly of the lack of any real desire to go on living in her current condition. My mother didn't want to cast herself into any big death scene either. She didn't want to inconvenience anyone. My mother had a great consideration for people. She even managed to die at about as convenient a time as it's possible to do such a thing.

Her doctor called me from the hospital at eight-thirty that evening. "Dr. Flavin?" he said.

"Yes."

"Your mother passed away half an hour ago."

"Oh," I said. And that was pretty much it.

Goodby, Ma, I thought. I had seen her just a few hours before, but she had not been conscious. So I had simply stood there, looking at her, at the face that was no longer hers, at the poor little shape beneath the bed covers to which she had finally been reduced. She had already been dead for me even then. But she had loved me as no other person could or would because she had been my mother, and was the only one of those I was ever going to have. My mother knew as much about love as my father, but dealt with it very differently. My father met it head on, arms wide. My mother just eased into it, letting it surround her, take her in. Which it did, without even a ripple. My mother disturbed nothing.

Do you think that's easy, Norman? I mean, to love and be loved and yet disturb nothing? Well, it isn't. By its very nature, love disturbs. It moves, it shakes, it causes people to act and things to happen. And most often, that's how it's used. But not by my mother. My mother never even tried to use it that way. In fact she never used it in *any* way. It was just there, sitting quietly beside her. And no one ever had to tell you. If you knew my mother, you knew it was there.

When I was a kid, my mother used to tell me stories while I ate, while she spooned eggs and other important foods I disliked into my mouth. I was a terrible eater. She was a wonderful story-teller. They were make-believe stories, but always with real people, always grounded in fact. The people were friends, cousins, aunts, uncles, enemies and allies. And I was always the hero, always the one who prevailed. I was a small, skinny kid, but in the stories my appearance was always deceptive because my mother gave me the strength of ten. I was never especially bright or precocious, but in my mother's Never-Never-Land I could outthink everyone. I hated eggs but loved my mother's stories. Why not? They made me feel twice blessed. For skinny little Robert Flavin, momma made all things seem possible.

And it didn't end with the stories. My mother was a great believer in love as a protective fortress. It was a theory she thought she had invented. She believed love was to protect, to cherish, to build, to pamper. Love was to keep the cold and the hurt outside, where they belonged. Inside the fortress was where they were never allowed. Not for a minute, not for any reason. Inside, there was no sitting in judgment, no hurt, no learning of harsh realities, no rejection, no teaching of tough lessons. All that took place *out*side, at the hands of others who took a twisted kind of pleasure in such things or whose job it was to teach. Inside the fortress was only for loving and for building of strength and confidence and the conviction that all things were possible if you truly believed them to be.

I was skinny, so my mother let me know that skinny was beautiful, much better than fat. But this never stopped her from trying to fatten me up a little. I was small for my age, so of course small was the thing to be. Didn't the best things always come in small packages? I was shy and not very aggressive, which meant that those who weren't, were obviously boorish and insensitive.

As time passed, of course, I was also being taught a few things outside my mother's fortress. I was learning that skinny *wasn't* always beautiful, especially not for football, wrestling, and general street fighting, in which I was regularly getting the bejesus knocked out of me. The same for small. Boy, you could sure keep *small* when it came to contact sports. And as for shyness and a lack of aggression, I was very quickly finding out that the meek may very well be inheriting the earth one day, but in the meantime all those common, boorish, insensitive sonsofbitches were grabbing just about everything in sight.

My mother remained unfazed by my complaints. Wait, she would tell me. If I'd wait, she said, I'd see how right she was. In this life, you had to be patient. What might seem wrong and bad at first, could later turn out right and good. I was young. I was just at the beginning of things. Life hadn't yet truly begun for me. What I was going through now, was merely the preparation for life. Wait, she told me, and I would see.

So I waited and I saw. And do you know something, Norman? My mother ended up with a pretty fair average. In time, by some miracle of genetics I still don't entirely understand, I actually grew tall. In an era of the obese, my early skinniness turned out to be a later blessing. It allowed me to mature into a slender fitness, while all those football players who trampled me were going to paunch and jowl. And I have no true regrets about my shyness either. I overcame it as I grew older, or at least managed to deal with it. And through most of my adult life, it gifted me with a range of insights I might not otherwise have had. You *must* remain apart and you *must* stand a little to one side to really see what's going on, to understand and feel what others may be feeling. If I've been at all effective in my work over the years, if I've been lucky enough to catch an occasional insight into human hurt that no medical text could offer, I believe much of it can be credited to that early, aching watchfulness of the outsider.

Which means my mother was right, if not always in specifics, then certainly in concept. Love *should* be a fortress. It *should* protect you from outside hurt. And it most certainly *should* help you believe all things are possible. This last, of course, has to be tempered with good judgment, because obviously *all* things are *not* possible. My mother knew this, while more than a few of my colleagues did not. And from time to time, some of their patient-victims in this area have stumbled into my office in the hope of redemption. Which is probably why we're all so busy in the shrink business, Norman. At least half of us are always furiously at work trying to patch up the mistakes of the other half.

One of these walking wounded, Lucy Feldor, once came to me as a patient after having withdrawn entirely from any part of the love arena. At the age of twenty-four, Lucy had formally announced her resignation from active male-female interplay. She was through with men, through with the battles of love and sex. She'd had enough. If she wanted to get hurt, she said, she might as well stay at home and just bang her head against the wall. The results would be no worse than the best she had ever gotten from men, and much less trouble.

Lucy was another of those confidence problems. She felt terribly insecure with and around men. She didn't think they liked her or found her at all attractive. And she was right. As she presented herself to them, there simply wasn't anything attractive about her. She was a walking "before" picture for Weight Watchers, Dale Carnegie, and Listerine all rolled into one. She was fat, had a hostile and overly aggressive personality (lack of confidence can cause aggression as often as meekness), and she was almost deliberately careless about her personal hygiene and dress.

But because she had been getting tired of rejection

and of feeling unloved, she had gone to one of my colleagues to have her confidence built up.

Her lack of confidence with men was certainly real enough, and her doctor treated it by using my mother's "fortress" theory, which he applied like a hot compress to a boil. Over long months of therapy, he worked to assure Lucy that she was really lovable, personable, and attractive, and that by keeping a strongly positive attitude, it was possible for her to attract any man she wanted. Which in itself was patently idiotic, because *no* woman can attract *any* man she may want, and certainly not Lucy. Reasonably sensible men and women, in seeking mates, shoot for those targets they feel they have at least a credible chance of hitting. What they don't do, unless they're utterly self-destructive, is shoot for the moon with a slingshot.

Yet Lucy's shrink now convinces her that if she can only learn to take strong affirmative action and believe in herself, armies of men will flock to her doorstep and camp there, panting. So that perched on a rocket of self-help clichés, Lucy blasts off. She goes out and makes an openly aggressive pass at the most desirable man in her office, the most sought after male prize in the place. But, what the hell, thinks Lucy. If her doctor says all things are possible and that she shouldn't just sit around waiting for men to come to *her*, then all things *were* possible.

So naturally she gets her poor head handed to her. She is not merely rejected, she is knocked flat, ridiculed, utterly humiliated. Now Lucy is in worse emotional shape than ever. But she keeps at it and hangs in there because that's what her doctor tells her to do. She doesn't wait for men to approach *her* as she once did. She goes after *them*. And not just ordinary run-of-the-mill guys. She goes after only the highest grade, the prime mating material, and is destroyed each time.

Finally, when her bleeding, suffering psyche can take no more, it rebels. "Enough!" it screams and will no longer let her out of the house. It forces her to her bed and keeps her there for a month. At the end of that time she comes to me, and I get *my* chance at her.

I'm obviously no miracle healer, Norman. You already know of some of my less brilliant efforts and there are unfortunately a lot more you *don't* know about. But I like to think not many of my efforts ever reached this particular level of incompetence. Not that I'm wholly unsympathetic to the doctor's intentions and premise. My mother's love-fortress concept is a basically sound one. To instill confidence and hope and self-esteem is a very positive approach. But it can't be applied simplistically and indiscriminately: certainly not in situations where all the harsh realities are working overtime against it. And unfortunately our mating rituals are subjected to the harshest realities.

In a practical sense, our love exchanges and the way they work can be reduced to a simple matter of product packaging and marketing. The more salable the product, the more appealing its design and wrapper, the broader its potential market and the higher its asking price is going to be. The most confident and aggressive sales pitch in the world isn't going to make a market success of an unattractive product. So the first thing I figured I'd better do with Lucy, even before I went to work on her bleeding psyche, was repackage her.

I made her lose thirty pounds. I had her get herself a more attractive hair style and well-fitting, fashionable clothes. And I insisted she do something about her personal hygiene. Enough with that negative rebellion, with that ridiculous insistence on the "natural" approach to grooming. There isn't much appeal to the human animal in its totally natural state. We're only bearable to one another when the odors and juices of living are being regularly washed away and scientifically restrained.

Next I went after her negative personality, her defensively cutting approach to people and things. "You're never going to be loved," I told her, "if you don't act more lovable yourself. You've got to stop attacking people and always putting them down." I even gave her one of my mother's favorite old homilies: "If you can't say anything nice to someone, don't say anything at all." Which of course wasn't easy for her. She was so accustomed to covering her insecurities with a tough sort of aggression that it had become almost instinctive. She met someone and instantly went on the attack. But when she finally did get the idea—and I had even taught her to smile as though she meant it and wasn't just grimacing to hide her dyspepsia—I sent her out into the love marketplace.

But I wasn't about to risk everything by getting her kicked in the face again. I wanted no more overmatching. She still wasn't about to captivate any male superstars. What my plan called for was someone who was her male counterpart in the love marketplace, a nice enough man, as Lucy was now a nice enough woman.

In time, with a little effort, Lucy found him. And she won him. And she grew to love him as he grew to love her. And with being loved, came confidence in her own appeal and lovability. Which in turn made her even more lovable. You know it as well as me, Norman. Things happen to work that way.

So with Lucy, I was lucky enough to be able to repair one more of my compadres' mistakes. The mating marketplace is a unique one and subject to all sorts of special variations, but its basic operating principles are no different from those of any other functioning market. It may sound cynical, but the laws of supply and demand are still in control, and you can only get what you can match in value. The medium of exchange varies, of course, and includes such things as looks, personality, intelligence, money, religion, educational and sociological background, worldly success and achievement, and something vague and mystical that we call sex appeal, although not necessarily in that order of importance. But it still means that a penniless, not especially bright, unskilled laborer has less chance of capturing a beautiful and wealthy Vassar graduate than he has of moving into a million-dollar estate in Connecticut. Our mating market guidelines are that rigid. Which in the long run, may well be best for all involved.

October 14

ONCE, NORMAN, I THINK it was just after Barbara and I were married, we went out for dinner one evening. We must have been celebrating something or other, because it was one of those perfect times when she and I and our entire world seemed right together. We were drinking some fine French wine that came in long, dark, graceful bottles, and we grew light and happy with it and with ourselves and danced to the kind of dreamy music that lets you just hold one another and not have to think about what your feet are doing. I looked at my shiny new wife, and there was a spotlight from somewhere touching her hair. It had the effect of a celestial glow, and I thought, my God, I've married an angel.

It was no true heavenly light, and Barbara was no angel. She was simply a particular grade of human, as was I, as are we all. But that still doesn't stop us from sometimes seeing halos and from sometimes putting them about the heads of those we love. Nor does it stop us, at other times, from seeing and putting horns on those very same heads. The fact that we have created them, have imagined them into being, doesn't matter. We take neither credit nor blame. We're sure it has nothing to do with us. It's always *them*. Only years later, if at all, do we sometimes get to see and accept the truth of it.

There was a period when I would have been willing to swear I had married the devil herself. My Barbara, I had decided, was evil, the princess of darkness, beyond redemption. That's the sort of nutty funk I had allowed myself to fall into. But I wasn't just any plain old nut, I was a *doctor* nut—a *shrink* nut—who, at the same time he was being a little paranoid himself, was busy treating the paranoia of others. It happens more often than we can ever be sure of knowing. It's a constant professional hazard—one of three. Sometimes we play God. Sometimes we're just ineffectually human. Sometimes we're quietly mad.

And our patients? Well, they just have to take their chances with us and hope they're lucky.

One of my less lucky patients, during that particular spell of darkness with Barbara, was a guy who came to me suffering from problems with his own wife. There he was, sitting across from me in my office, bleeding from the heart and mind, pouring out his laundry list of injustices, detailing all the devilish things his wife was doing to him, while I sat soaking in each detail. But instead of just listening with the cool, professional detachment that was properly expected of me, I was filled with such bitterness, such overt malice towards his wife, my wife, and all wives, living and dead, that I practically cheered him on.

Why, that bitch! How could a woman *do* that to her own husband? Where's her love, her loyalty? Can't she ever think of anyone but herself? She should be taught a lesson. She should be thrown out on her ungrateful, narcissistic ass.

Although I didn't actually say these things, I was thinking them and my attitude all but implied them. I was sitting in judgment. I was the husband's ally. I stood shoulder to shoulder *with* the husband, *against* the wife, when I had no business being for or against either one. And if there was even a faint chance of survival for my patient's marriage *before* he walked into my office, there was no chance at all after he got there. I wasn't about to let this poor, abused, long-suffering husband, this latter-day Job of the matrimonial state, take any more abuse from that miserable wretch he was living with.

So, in my secret madness, I struck at my own wife and all wives through my patient and his wife, and had the bitter satisfaction of seeing both our marriages go up in smoke within a few months of one another. Who knows? If the guy had come to me during a more hopeful period in my love life, he might still have been married.

Yet, sad and bad as the case was, it wasn't really that unusual. It happens often enough for us even to have given it a name. We call it countertransference. And it means that as therapists, we're sometimes inescapably affected by the feelings—the irritations, the prejudices, the passions—that make us the people we are under our professional titles. We're not just hunks of medical machinery, Norman. I have wept for my patients. I have been angered by them, I have liked them, I have even loved them. We do our best not to get involved this way, but aren't always successful. Sometimes we don't even know we're involved. Other times we know, but can't help ourselves. And occasionally, we know but choose *not* to help ourselves.

I once indulged myself in this last—I once chose *not* to help myself with a patient named Betty Stieron. This also happened during that same bad period with Barbara. I'm not trying to excuse myself by bringing my wife into it. I don't think I even *want* to excuse myself. I just mention it as background. But I'm sure my behavior in this case also had to be affected by what was happening at home.

Betty was an attractive urbane woman in her early thirties when she first appeared in my office as a patient. She worked as an editor for one of the major fashion magazines, was good at her job, popular with men, and had enough humor and personality for three. She was also in a quiet but complete state of panic about her love life.

Her case was pretty much of a classic in its symptoms and background. About ten years earlier, she had been shoved into a car by three young animals and raped and sodomized repeatedly over a twelve-hour period. For a long time after the attack, she couldn't bear to have a man even touch her. Later, she overcame this initial revulsion enough to at least permit herself occasional attempts at making love. But even the attempts themselves were bad. She was totally uptight from beginning to end and could never relax enough to get any true pleasure from it. And instead of getting better, it was beginning to feed on itself and grow worse. Until it reached the point where she even stopped trying, she even stopped permitting herself to attempt love entirely.

She did, occasionally, still go out with men. She enjoyed them as people, as company. Sometimes she even cared about them. But when a relationship approached the bedroom stage, she would create some story, make up some excuse and back away from it. She could never allow herself to explain adequately what her problem was. She was too ashamed of it. As a result she went through one searingly miserable experience after another.

She was in especially bad emotional shape when she came to me. Therapy wasn't new to her. She had already been to three different shrinks in five years, which didn't project any brilliant hopes for success with me. When a patient comes to me with this kind of history of shrink-hopping, I know I'm in for a hard time. By then, most of them are convinced they know as much about psychotherapy as you and a lot more about their own unique and specific problems. And sometimes they do. They have all the required jargon down pat, anticipate each of your approaches and moves, and take a sinister delight in second guessing you right down the line. They literally *dare* you to try to help them. Their attitude says, all those other money-grubbing quacks couldn't help me worth a damn and I spent years with them. What makes you think *you* can?

But in this case, Betty and I had something good going for us right from the start. I liked her instantly and she seemed to react the same way to me. This happens in therapy and out of it. As I said, we can't help responding as the people we are under our official robes. And Betty happened to be an exceptionally appealing young woman. She had warmth, sensitivity, an ability to laugh at herself, and a particular lack of self-pity that touched me right off. Also, she had the soft hurt eyes of a wounded doe, dying quietly of a hunter's bullet and knowing it, but not having the faintest understanding of why.

I swear, Norman, sometimes when she looked at me, smiling, but with the silent terror of her loneliness plucking at me from her eyes, she could quite manage to tear me apart. God, how I wanted to help her then, wanted to hold and comfort her, wanted to soothe, wanted to offer whatever balm my brain, heart, and loins might carry.

Yes, my loins too. That also happens. What you want to give, you want to *give*. And Betty was starting to feel the same way. I had been seeing her three times a week through the better part of a year, through an entire fall, winter, and spring. She trusted me. She shared every thought, every tear, every hurt, every joy with me as she had shared them with no other man in her life. And I? Well, I was thinking of how much more pleasant it was to listen to the soft warmth of *her* voice rather than the harsh, shrill carping of Barbara's—to see the open admiration, the respect on *her* face, instead of the increasingly negative judgment on Barbara's—to breathe the sweet longing for me coming off her like flowers, instead of getting hit by the cold blasts of my wife's rejection.

I found myself looking forward like a kid to my scheduled time with Betty, and digging for excuses not to go home to Barbara. Very simply, Norman, what I felt towards my wife during these months was pure malice, and what I felt for my patient was a real kind of love.

I kissed Betty one afternoon. By then it seemed a natural enough thing to do. It was just after what had been an especially good session for us and we both felt it. We had done something good together. She was lovely, she was close, she was needing. And so was I. In fact I needed everything about her, including *her* need of *me*. Still, I felt myself shocked when it happened. I was shaking. I felt as I imagined a priest might feel on breaking his vow of celibacy. No different. As one of St. Sigmund's holy apostles, I had indeed sinned, had indeed betrayed one of our religion's most sacred tenets. I had actually touched, had actually embraced a patient.

Betty handled it better than I. We looked at one another, and she told me she loved me. God, those three words can have power and magic in them. Especially when you're hearing them for the first time from someone you care about. And what did I do in response to those three magical words? I explained to her as coolly, pedantically, and stupidly as I was able, that I understood, that it wasn't that unusual a thing, that it often happened between patient and therapist, and that we in the profession had ways of dealing with it. Except that Betty didn't *want* to deal with it. And for that matter, neither did I. What we wanted to do was take advantage of it—each for our own reasons.

Still, I did make a reasonable effort to play my properly ethical role. I said, "Listen, darling . . ." Now isn't that a great beginning, Norman, for someone trying to impersonalize a relationship, to cool things off? "Darling," I said, "you've got to understand. You may think it's real, but it's only a touch of transference. I'm here. I'm helping you. You're grateful. You feel close to me. You feel trusting. I'm a man. You're a woman. We're involved with one another on a regular basis." I tried all that.

Her answer was succinct. "Bullshit."

I laughed.

"Don't laugh," she said. "I mean it."

"I'm just trying to help you."

"I know. But if you really want to help me, then love me and let me love you. And most of all, *make* love to me."

I just looked at her.

"I feel I could with you," she said. "I wouldn't be afraid. I know it would be right and good."

But I couldn't be honest even then, Norman. I had to go through the rest of our catalog of stock denials. I had to explain that a therapist just didn't do that sort of thing; that besides being unethical, it would be bad for her. Incidentally, this last was a lie. In fact,

I thought it would be great for her at this time. I thought, all right, she *wants* to make love with me because she trusts and feels something for me. Then once she's able to let go enough with *me* to truly enjoy the experience, once she finds out it *can* be as wonderful as it was meant to be, she might be able to carry over the attitude and sensation to other men.

I also thought I loved her, wanted her, and would delight in going to bed with her. And finally, I thought I deserved her as some kind of moral payment for what I was going through with Barbara. It was my *right*, damn it! I was dying at home, carrying my secret madness. Betty could help preserve my sanity, could guide me back to an even keel. For me to love her and for her to love me would be a two-way blessing.

I was very thoughtful, you see, Norman, for a man whose mind had stopped working.

But I carried on my little charade of protests through a few more therapy sessions—at least until the time when I suppose my conscience was soothed enough, my ethical conditioning subdued enough for me to be convinced I had given us both enough warnings. Then I allowed *her* to draw *me* into bed, like a child leading a reluctant adult into a new kind of game she had invented. And what marvelous therapy for us both, Norman, even in retrospect. She was so eager by then, so parched, that she held back nothing. She wanted everything she had been missing. And as for me, it was like an emotional transfusion at a time when I needed exactly that sort of strengthening.

So, am I making a brief for a therapist contributing himself body and soul to the needs of a patient if he thinks it's going to help the therapy? Hardly. All I'm saying is that it happened this way for me this particular time, and that it's not as uncommon a happening as the profession would like the public to believe. Although the public is starting to smarten up as more and more of these cases break into the news. Even some of our own psychological associations have begun talking openly about it at their meetings. A few years ago, the subject would never have even been brought up. Any mention of emotional or sexual relationships between therapists and patients was considered *verboten.* They were regarded as the hairline cracks in our foundations that could one day bring the entire psychotherapeutic structure tumbling down on our heads. Now the discussions focus not on *whether* such relationships exist, but on how often they may occur and how they may affect those involved. Is it good for the patient, we ask, or bad for the patient? What does it do to the therapy and the therapist? And what about the husbands and wives of those caught up in it?

Apart from all the other considerations, just imagine the wear and tear on the busy therapist. Personally, I happen to think the whole concept of such relationships can spell only disaster for psychotherapy and those involved in it. Never mind about Betty and me. Never mind what I did. Even that was all wrong. It was just something I needed, wanted, and was willing to indulge myself in at the time. As for Betty, all it did was quickly put an end to any possibility of further therapy from me. Once we were lovers, how honest could she be with me about her other relationships? And to whom could she go for a clinical discussion about *me*? It was no good. And when she realized what a dead end we were in, even the sexual pleasure faded for her. Not to mention the guilt she felt at having seduced me away from my sacred vows of professional celibacy.

I tried, but it didn't help to tell her it was *I* who did the seducing, not she. It was somehow impossible for her to believe that—not a high-type, dedicated professional like me, not a *doctor*, for God's sake! All she hoped for, finally, was that I could forgive her, not think too harshly of her. Imagine that. Well, I forgive you, Betty, with your dark, lovely, wounded-doe eyes. I loved you and I don't think harshly of you at all.

Nor do I think harshly of the more than several others I may have also permitted to seduce me in the line of duty over the years. Worse things than love have happened to them and to me.

One of these women was named Jenny, and in this case, Norman, I won't even try to justify it by pointing to my troubles with Barbara. It took place after our divorce, when I was floating free. So this one was all mine.

Jenny was a hooker. Not one of your ordinary run-of-the-mill whores who pluck their johns off the sidewalks for ten or twenty bucks. My Jenny worked only by referral, charged a minimum fee of a hundred dollars, and often got as much as five hundred to a thousand for a weekend jaunt. She was a true jet-set hooker, with clients in many different parts of the country and exquisitely engraved business cards that read, "Have Body, Will Travel." She had humor too.

Jenny was graduated *cum laude* from a good Midwestern university, had a masters degree in philosophy, and was probably as much a victim of her intelligence as others are of their lack of it. Too impatiently clever for her own good, she found life's more ordinary paths dull beyond bearing. In whatever she did, she pushed for originality of concept, uniqueness of design, and brilliance of performance. With the result that she was one of the most exciting and charming women I've ever known, and one of the most psychologically screwed up.

An always fascinating part of my work, Norman, is the insights it offers into the random events that affect our lives out of all proportion to their seeming importance at the time they take place. In Jenny's case it was seeing the moving picture "Klute" that apparently tipped the scale in favor of her ultimate choice of careers. I don't know if you've seen the picture, Norman, but it features Jane Fonda in the role of a most unusual and attractive hooker named Bree, who is complex enough to have mixed emotions about what she does and is undergoing some form of psychotherapy because of it.

Seeing the movie, Jenny immediately empathized with Bree. She found the portrayed image of the movie hooker exciting. "Her work gave her such marvelous control over men," was how she once described it. "She was always the one in command. It was beautiful." So Jenny had her stimulus and inspiration and was ready for them. She was out of college, jobless, bored, and without direction. She had come of age at a time when sex was regarded as a popular form of entertainment, and she considered herself without peer as an entertainer. She was neither more nor less promiscuous than most of the girls she knew from college, but this still left her plenty of room for action. "Unless your date was a real creep," she said, "you usually ended up in bed with him. Why not? It was usually what we both wanted, so why play games?"

That was the sexual climate in which Jenny functioned as an amateur. Emotional involvement played little or no part in it, so the jump from sex for fun to sex for pay wasn't really that big. It was just a question of interest, timing, and opportunity. Jane Fonda had already aroused Jenny's interest, boredom made the timing right, and the opportunity arrived late one night when she was alone in a bar after telling her date to go to hell. When a man approached, she pretended to be a pro then actually carried the joke through. Finding the experience painless and intriguing, she went on from there. "It wasn't really that much different from dating," she said. "It was just that the men were usually a little older, richer, and kinkier."

Jenny came to me after having been a working girl for several years. Like many patients, she denied the need for therapy even while she sought and received it. She claimed she had started with me as a joke—as she had also started hooking as a joke. Which was obviously her way of easing into things she might otherwise have found difficult. "Hell!" she once laughed. "Bree had a shrink, so why shouldn't I?" And since Bree had also found it necessary to seduce the straight, young investigator who had intruded in her life, the next logical step in Jenny's progression was to try to seduce *me*.

I must admit, Norman, she was one damned good little seducer. She had a sensually lovely face, an incomparable body, and a way of moving and positioning herself that would have made a brilliant textbook study in female eroticism. Add to this a series of minutely detailed descriptions of her more exotic professional talents, and you have some idea of what I was up against. After a few months, she abandoned whatever small subtleties still remained and brought it all out into the open.

"What's the matter?" she asked at one point. "Don't I appeal to you?"

"Why is that so important?" I said.

"I'm not sure. Maybe professional pride. Maybe I want to show you how great I am. Maybe you appeal to me as a man. Maybe because you're my shrink and traditionally taboo. Or maybe a little of each." She smiled. "Have you ever been to bed with a pro?"

"No," I told her.

"Aren't you the least bit curious?"

I shrugged. "There are just so many possible variations on any given theme."

"Maybe. But there's also the question of talent."

"Professionals have no monopoly on that," I said.

"That's what I thought too when I did it for fun. I thought I was great. And for an amateur, I probably was. But don't kid yourself, Doc. A pro is still a pro. In *anything*." She smiled at me with perfect teeth. "If you're worried about my prices, don't be. I wouldn't charge you."

"Why not?" I asked.

"Professional courtesy."

"I'd still charge *you*," I told her.

"I'd expect you to," she said. "Doctors are a lot greedier than whores."

It became an on-going thing. She called it Operation Shrink and spent much of each session on the campaign. It was her time and she could talk about anything she wished, but it finally seemed to be getting counterproductive. One day I called this to her attention and told her to try and remember why she was there.

She considered it. "Maybe this *is* why I'm here."

"You mean to get *me* into bed?" I said.

"Is that really so weird a motive?" she asked.

"Not if it's true," I said. "*Is* it?"

"I think so," she said. "At least, *now*. At the beginning I came because it seemed *de rigueur* to have a shrink. And after all, what was a brilliant, educated, exceptional doll like me doing as a whore anyway? Chasing kicks was obviously too simplistic an answer. It had to go deeper than that. So I decided to treat myself to some high-class professional digging. I've never really believed in psychotherapy anyway. And now that I'm in it, I'm still not convinced it's anything but a bore."

"A lot of things seem to bore you," I said.

"*You* don't, Doc."

"If I went to bed with you, I soon would," I said.

She grinned. "Let's try it and see."

But she wasn't always so light, Norman. There were times when my refusal to take the bait frustrated and angered her. Once, she said, "My God, you're a superior sonofabitch!"

I didn't say anything. Getting the anger out was good.

"Look at you!" she said. "You sit there in that big, goddamned chair as if it were a royal throne."

"Would it make you feel better if I sat in a smaller chair?" I asked.

"Up yours," she said. "I suppose you think that precious thing of yours would be contaminated if it were ever so much as touched by a whore."

I sat looking at her. Her face was flushed, her eyes bright, her body soft and vulnerable, and I thought, very unprofessionally, my God, what a woman.

"Well, let me tell you something, Your Royal Psychiatrist," she said. "We're *all* whores in this world. We *all* peddle little pieces of ourselves. And whether it's our brains, guts, or asses we're hustling, it's all the same. And though I realize you're a very high-class type of medical person, *you're* a whore too. For fifty bucks an hour, you peddle interest and sympathy when you don't really give a damn. And because you're dealing with the absolute heart of where we live, you're the worst whore of all."

"Don't you think I give a damn about you?" I asked. She had worked herself to the point of tears and was beginning to reach me.

"The only thing you give a damn about," she wept, "is your lousy fifty bucks."

"That's not fair," I said.

"Do you think it's fair to treat me as though I were something unclean?"

"Oh, come on, Jenny."

"A leper!" she cried. "You'd think I was a goddamned leper!"

"That's foolish," I told her.

"Is it?" she said and got out of her chair and dropped to her knees before me. "Then for God's sake, let me see if you can at least *touch* me without feeling revulsion."

I put my hand on her shoulder. She looked at me with wet eyes, then covered my hand with hers, and moved it to her breast. "Does it really feel so disgusting?"

I didn't say anything. Neither did I move my hand.

"I'm not dirt," she wept. She was holding me then and I felt her wet cheek. She was also doing other things, which I was aware of but utterly unwilling to stop. You can reach a point sexually, Norman, where you become so deliciously anesthetized by pleasure that even if the brain goes on screaming its warnings, you just don't give a damn.

Afterward she cooed happily, a mother soothing her cranky child. I almost expected her to say, there, there, darling. She was that pleased, that content. But she didn't say anything. She was waiting for me to speak. It was taking me time to get myself rounded up and stuck together. My hands and knees were still shaking. Christ, Norman! And all right there in my office with my goddamned nurse sitting just outside the door. "All right," I sighed at last, then sat very still as she licked my ear. "So a pro's a pro."

It was hardly the romance of the century, but we did have something nice going for a few months. And unusual for us both. I was Jenny's first and only shrink, and she was my first and only hooker. When she finally left my professional as well as my not-so-professional ministrations, it was for a rich Greek with yachts, villas, and Aegean Islands.

I heard from her only once. About six months after she left, I received a post card from an oil-rich emirate on the Persian Gulf. It said, "Hi, Shrink! The Arabs seem to be inheriting *me* right along with the rest of the earth. But it's all so *boring....* Real, real love, Your Jenny."

I'm glad Jenny happened to me, Norman. Wherever I've gone since, I've never found her anything but delightful to look back upon.

October 16

I'VE BEEN NOTICING SOMETHING, Norman. I seem to keep addressing you as Norman on these tapes instead of just the abbreviated, less formal Norm. Did I always call you Norman? I mean, when we spoke in person? I can't seem to remember anymore. It suddenly bothers me. I'd hate to think I was formalizing this in any way. As I said a while back, we're all such terrible hams. Maybe these tapes are just my own way of sneaking in a nice long third act all for myself.

I'd like to look at it for a minute. I think it's clear enough to us both by now that these tapes are more for me than they could possibly be for you. I obviously must need them—both as something to do with my heavier moments and as a kind of record. One of our major conceits as humans is believing that each of us is unique in thought and experience. And I suppose we are, which in itself can be frightening because this separates us from one another even further.

What I'm trying to say, Norman, what I'm apparently groping for in these tapes, is a recorded expression of my own uniqueness in the area of love. What I'm saying, in essence, is "Listen to me! I'm Robert Flavin, the only such person ever to have lived. Listen to what my life has taught me about human love."

How's that for arrogance? But is it actually any more arrogant than the implied attitudes of writers and lecturers like yourself, who keep turning out books and pontificating to the world on just about every subject? As though *your* words were the true and definitive ones and must be read and heard and preserved for all time? No, Norman. I don't believe my sin of arrogance is really any greater than yours. So I'm not going to apologize for it.

Yet, everyone has their own life's substance, so what do they need with mine? And since everyone also has their own thoughts about love, they probably don't care about mine. Or maybe they do.

Because I once had someone very close to me, Norman—my grandfather, in fact—who didn't seem to care much about my thoughts or about the substance of my life either. And it turned out very differently. So, let me tell you about it.

I guess I must have been around eight when my mother's father came to live with us. My mother was the youngest and poorest of her brothers and sisters, so naturally she got stuck with the old man. My aunts and uncles contributed to his support, and my parents needed the money, but that wasn't why they took him in when he grew too old and feeble to live alone. I guess my mother loved him. I say guessed, because I wasn't sure of such things in those days. I rarely heard the word used as such. Also, my grandfather never struck me as being especially lovable. I remember him as an unsmiling, mostly silent old man with a long white beard that was stained yellow from tobacco. He looked little different to me from any number of other old Jewish men in those days, with their black coats and hats and high, squeaky shoes. One orthodox old man always seemed interchangeable with another.

My grandfather appeared to speak no English, I spoke no Yiddish, and neither of us seemed to care about that fact. We had nothing to say to one another anyway. I was always dashing out to play or to school, he was either reading or praying at home or at the synagogue up the block, and we were rarely in the same room together. If I was out in the street with the kids and he happened to shuffle past, there was no sign of recognition from either of us. I don't think any of the kids even knew he was my grandfather. Which was okay with me, because I was kind of ashamed of him anyway. What could an old greenhorn of a grandpa possibly add to my All-American status on the block? And I figured he was ashamed of me too, since he never so much as glanced in my direction as he passed. When he slipped and fell one day at the synagogue and had to be carried back to our apartment by a small cortege of dark-suited men, I carefully looked the other way and went on with the more important business of my punchball game. The whole thing was just too embarrassing.

He never passed by any of my ball games again. He had broken his hip when he fell, and after he returned from the hospital, the only time he ever left the house again was to be buried. After he was hurt, he spent his time either in bed or in a wheelchair. Sometimes when he was asleep, I'd stop at the door to his room and look at his face. I had never really looked at him before and it felt strange. I thought he looked remarkably like an old pirate I had seen in a movie.

One afternoon he opened his eyes and saw me staring at him, and I felt as though I had been caught in a shameful act. I started to turn away, but he motioned me closer to his bed and took my hand. It was the first time he had ever touched me. He held my hand for a long time while I stood there, not knowing where to look or what to do. Finally, he smiled. I don't think I had ever seen him smile before. "It's all right, *boychikel*," he said. "I love you."

The words were barely audible, but I understood them. They were mostly *English*, for God's sake! And for some reason I couldn't understand then, I started to cry.

I came to stay with him in his room every day after that. Some days I didn't even go out to play. I had started to talk to my grandfather, and once I started, it was impossible to stop. I just talked and talked. I don't know how much he understood, but he listened carefully to everything I said and nodded and seemed to smile in all the right places. There was a softness in his eyes, in those amber irises I had inherited, and I loved to look into them. He spoke to me too, in a mixture of Yiddish and English that I somehow managed to piece together. If you want to enough, you can understand anything.

But my grandfather was dying. His organs were failing in successive stages and his faculties were slowly starting to go with them. I don't know whether I really understood what was happening. The true concept of death comes late to us. But I do know I didn't want to leave his side. When I wasn't in school, there was suddenly nothing else I wanted to do more than bring him his food, feed him when that became necessary, and even help keep him clean when it came to that.

My mother at first tried to get me to go outside and play more. It wasn't healthy to hang around inside so much. But when I resisted and she saw how it was, she left it alone.

Unfortunately I came to know and love my grandfather only as he began to die. And although I was very young at the time, I should have learned something from the experience. But I apparently didn't, and as an adult and a doctor, I have even managed to put my lack of learning about the process of dying to specific use in my practice. How? By advising my patients to dispatch their elderly, ailing, and infirm to those characteristic mid-twentieth-century phenomena, to those stinking pestholes of the unwanted and the dying, to those human refuse dumps we call nursing homes.

I've told my patients burdened with ailing loved ones that sending them to nursing homes would be best for everyone. Their elderly beloved, I've said, would get competent, professional care, they themselves would be spared being turned into nurses and orderlies, and their households wouldn't have to be ruptured by the depressing presence of a constantly demanding invalid. And I'm not the only doctor, shrink or otherwise, who has been giving such advice. Almost all of us do. Why? Because some of us are stupid enough to truly believe in it, and the rest know it's what our patients want and need to hear to soothe their poor aching consciences. It's just another of the opiates we dispense along with our tranquilizers and antidepressants. We want to keep everything nice and clean and antiseptic—no stink of urine in the home, no cries of hurt and fear, no quarreling about whose turn it may be to get stuck with the old one next.

So we exile our dying to our own ice floes, the nursing homes, and advise our patients to do the same with theirs. My wife willingly cleaned up after a puppy she was housebreaking, but was horrified and furious at once having to do the same for my mother when the old lady's failing bladder betrayed her in our dining room. I should have known better, but I felt pretty much as Barbara did. Who needed it, I thought, and sent the old lady off for some really competent professional care.

So I asked myself who needed it, and although I knew the answer, I wouldn't accept it. Because it's pretty clear by now that we all need it, *all* of us. Increasingly, we seem to be confused by love. We forget what it means. We think it's just another form of entertainment. We want to trot it out for our pleasure, then have it removed the minute it stops being fun. We establish cut-off points for age and health. When it gets to be too unpleasant or too much trouble to love, we dig up reasons not to go on with it. But of course we can't admit to such a thing. How could we say we don't love our parents or grandparents anymore because they've become too old or too sick or too much of a nuisance? So what we say instead is that it would be better for everyone concerned if we just shunted the old folks out of sight somewhere to do their dying.

Except that it's not better, Norman. It's worse for the elderly, who feel unloved, abandoned, and alone among strangers at the very time they're least able to cope with such feelings. It's worse for the middle-aged, who are usually responsible for putting them in that position and who must carry the guilt along with the bitter knowledge that they're going to get pretty much the same treatment when their own turn comes. And it's certainly worse for the young, who are not only being shown a pathetic absence of love at an impressionable age, but are being led to believe that dying, instead of being a natural part of the life cycle, is so frightening, obscene, and terrible that it must be kept locked away from everything else.

We allow our elderly to live longer, but ensure

that they enjoy it less. And when they're about to leave, we give them a final boot in the ass so they'll know exactly how we feel about their going. And as doctors, we deserve blame on all counts. The process of dying is part of our business. We work with it on a daily basis. We set the patterns for the attitudes surrounding it. If we treat our dying without compassion or love, if we regard them as burdensome, broken-down machines to be tossed on the scrap pile as efficiently and antiseptically as possible, so will everyone else. And we're doing it, Norman.

But when I was eight years old, my mother let me do it differently. She let me stay with and help care for my grandfather to the end. The fact that I wasn't able to hold onto and use what I learned after I became a doctor was my own fault, not hers. She did all she could to see that I had good and proper instruction in the way those things should work. And my grandfather also turned out to be a superlative teacher. The first words he ever spoke to me were of love and so were the last. During the eight months in between, which was about all the time we were to have together, he showed me how love between the old and the young was supposed to work. He listened to me, he spoke to me, and he looked at me with his amber irises. He let me know he cared about my thoughts and about the substance of my life. He let me know this in a hundred ways, most of which I no longer remember, and in a single way I've never forgotten.

I was reading the newspaper to him one afternoon a few weeks before he died. I don't know how much of the English he understood. Probably very little. But he used to enjoy just listening to my voice and to the words. He liked my voice. He said it had the sound of a young bird. I could feel him looking at me as I read, and every so often I would look back at him and smile. He'd sort of nod then, which was almost like a smile, and I'd start reading once more. When he seemed to be asleep after a while, I put down the paper and walked quietly towards the door.

"*Boychikel,*" he said, which means little boy and was what he always called me.

I went back and stood beside his bed. He reached into one of the pockets of his robe and took out his watch. It was a heavy old brass watch with a cover you had to snap open to see the time. It had been a gift from his own grandfather on his thirteenth birthday and he had carried it ever since. There was a gold chain attached, with a small pocket knife at the other end. He put the watch and chain and knife in my hand and closed my fingers around them. Then he smiled.

I looked at him and didn't understand.

"*Deine,*" he said. "Yours."

Suddenly afraid, I shook my head.

"Yours," he said again.

"No grandpa," I told him. "It's not mine. I don't want it. It's yours." I wanted to shove the watch back in his pocket and run. But I couldn't move. For the first time in my life I had felt that inevitable chill that precedes a final parting. I didn't know enough to understand it, but I knew enough to be frightened.

He understood. "Don't be afraid."

Something was clotted in my throat. Not only couldn't I move, I couldn't speak.

"Is good," he said, meaning the watch, and made a motion towards his ear. "You listen."

I managed to get the watch up as far as my ear and heard the good, strong, steady beat of it.

"Good?" he said.

I nodded. I still had no voice.

"Yours," he said. "For *your boychikel.*"

He had pushed me two generations ahead. I somehow began to feel better. In a few words, he had managed to give me a feeling of continuity. It was all there, right in the watch. I would be a grandpa too, one day, and I would have this good watch to give to my own little boy. Nothing really ended. This was what he was trying to tell me.

I still have the watch, Norman. I won't be able to give it to my own grandson, but maybe my son will, although that's not quite the same thing. Or maybe I can manage to buy myself a small piece of continuity with these tapes. Maybe *they* can be my grandpa's watch.

October 18

I FIND MYSELF THINKING more and more about Barbara these days, Norman. And sometimes I feel sorry
for her, which would bother her terribly if she knew.
She would despise even the idea that there could
possibly be anything about her to arouse sympathy.
And that in itself is probably the saddest and most
touching thing of all.

My wife is an instant public optimist. Alone, she
might be uncertain, depressed, and filled with fears.
But let just one other person come into sight—loved
one, stranger, friend or enemy, it doesn't matter—
and she's instantly confident, happy, and positive
about all things. She feels compelled to appear per-

fect, without a blemish, and it's not easy. In fact it's very hard, not only for her, but for anyone who cares about her. And I care about her.

We were crazy about each other. We couldn't wait to be alone together, to touch, to grab, to talk or just to look. It was that strong, even after we were married. But even more important, we *liked* each other. Whatever we did together was fun. Barbara used to tease me about my work then too, but it was a nice teasing, a warm, loving teasing. She'd say how lucky she was to be married to such a smart person, an all-knowing shrink, a man of science who knew so much about people, who understood everything about what they did and why they did it. And how flattering that of all women, I had chosen *her*, since this meant, of course, that she must be something special herself. No woman could possibly deceive a man of my insights.

At that time, Norman, I believe my wife really loved what I was and what I did. She not only felt pride in me but pride in herself for having captured such a shining prize. My God, was I wonderful! It even added spice to our lovemaking for her. If I knew all things about the human mind and body, then I knew better than anyone what would titillate, excite, tease, please, and satisfy a woman sexually, and she could only assume that what I was offering her in bed was the absolute best.

Barbara has been proven wrong in many of her assumptions over the years, but never more wrong than she was in that particular one. In those days, I was actually a lousy lover, at least, judged by current standards. And most of the blame for that was specifically *because* of the profession in which Barbara took such pride. During those early days of my career there was no stronger influence in my life than Freud's teachings. I was a true apostle. Anything he had said, I accepted without question. And one of the things I accepted blindly and unquestioningly was Freud's contention that women were intended to be, should be, and in fact *were* the passive sex. If a woman was forward in any way, this was to be regarded as a specifically male trait and a positive sign of some sort of neurosis.

So since Freud believed it, I believed it. And I wasn't alone in the profession. The concept was pretty rampant in psychiatric circles. I believe it still is, though to a lesser degree. Offhand, I can't think of a single woman who is head of a psychiatry department in a medical school, which surely must say *something* about our attitude toward women.

But as far as I was concerned then, the concept was very quickly injected into my bloodstream and incorporated into my cells. I may not have always been aware of it, but it was there. It affected everything I had to do with women generally and with Barbara specifically. And it surely affected her appeal for me right from the start. My wife is a small, slender, delicately made woman, Norman, the archetypical female image. I always loved her *petite* quality. I adored it. I called her my little Dresden doll. My God! And I had even read Ibsen. Barbara was rather shy then, too, hesitant about speaking out on controversial topics and never in open opposition to me. Which I also adored—naturally. Who wanted a big, brash, loud-mouthed, fishmonger's wife for a beloved? Not I. Of course the possibility of something in between a fish-monger's wife and a Dresden doll never even oc-curred to me. Being a man of extremes, I knew no middle ground and certainly not in bed. Here was the deepest and broadest male-female separation of all. And I expected no deviations, not that Barbara would have been likely to deviate and put me to the test. She was always eager and willing, but never aggres-sive. She never refused my sexual advances, but never initiated any either. If she had, I wouldn't have liked it. According to my rigidly Freudian concept of the female sexual image, it would have been too male-oriented. Aggressive women in bed had always turned me off and Barbara knew it. That sort of action be-longed to whores and neurotic, sexually confused females. My poor wife wasn't even allowed to climb on top of me. Heaven forbid! A female in the posi-tion of ascendancy? That sort of unfitting behavior not only didn't go, but wasn't even considered. Down, girl! Stay where all good, truly female little women belonged. *Underneath.*

That should give you some idea, Norman, of what a great lover I must have been in those days. And how well qualified to guide my patients through whatever problems they may have had with their own sexual games. I'm surprised none of them ever came after me when they finally learned what I'd been doing to them. Maybe they just never learned.

Maybe they just went on and on, believing good little females never initiated sexual advances and never climbed on top.

But Barbara learned. Not quickly and not from me, but she learned. It came hard for both of us. And it wasn't only about sex that she learned. She literally conceived of equal rights for women all by herself. She stopped being my little Dresden doll. She stopped being especially proud of me and of my profession. She stopped thinking I knew everything about all things. And I hated it.

The thing was, Norman, I knew she was right. But I needed the adoration. It wasn't easy for me to give it up, at least not without a fight. So we fought, and we hurt each other. I thought I knew so much and I knew absolutely nothing. I took refuge in Freud. I wrapped his theories around me like a child's security blanket, but all they did was isolate me and drive me further away from Barbara.

Now I sometimes try to imagine what I'd do differently with her if I had the chance. And I think what I'd do first is carefully forget everything about love that St. Sigmund ever taught me. I'd keep my arms wide, my heart open, and my brain under strict control. And how I'd love her then! How I'd appreciate what we had. I wouldn't pick it apart, bit by bit. I wouldn't keep expecting, expecting. And I swear, Norman, I'd even say to hell with Freud and let her climb on top.

That getting on top seems to have really stuck in my mind. It's just a symbol, of course, but an important one. Actually, Barbara never even wanted it that

way. She preferred me dominant in bed. It was my
need, rather than the fact itself, that was the problem.
I always had to feel in control in everything. I've
never even allowed myself to get really drunk because
it would mean a certain loss of control. And I've led
my life accordingly. Why do you think being a psychiatrist had such appeal? I was always in command—
the controller, the manipulator, the God player. But
when you played God all day in the office, it wasn't
easy to stop when you got home.

Maybe I should have allowed myself to get drunk
once in a while, Norman. Maybe then I'd have been
better at loving her, at letting her know how I felt.
I had such a damn big mouth most of the time. I was
so great at telling people things. Why should it have
been so hard for me to tell her I was sorry, I was
wrong, I needed her?

A silly rhetorical question, of course. I know the
answers. It's my business to know. Only I could never
accept it for myself. I told you before, Norman, that
Barbara had to appear perfect. Well, I was just as
bad in that respect. No. I was worse because I knew
all the psychological tricks. I could carry the whole
thing off better. So naturally I had to be *super-*
perfect. And if I was, how could I ever admit to being
wrong? Or say I was sorry? Or say I need you, when
it was obvious that anyone as perfect as me didn't need
anyone?

Except that I did need her. But the only time I ever
told her was when she couldn't hear.

It was during an illness she was going through a
long time ago. It was a bad one, with everything go-

ing wrong, and there was a strong chance she might not come out of it. I was frightened for her and stayed at the hospital through all one night. I sat in her room and looked at the walls and the furniture and her sleeping face. She was under heavy sedation, and she never moved at all. She looked gone to me. Her flesh seemed already to have the pale, stiff look of the dead.

My stomach felt cold and sick, but it felt that way less for her than for myself. If she died, she would be gone and that would be the end of it for her. But it wouldn't be the end for me. I'd have to go home to our house, our room, our bed and she wouldn't be there. I'd remember her when she was twenty-two and beautiful and hear her laughing and saying things that no one else has ever said to me in quite the same way. I'd remember her the day we were married, and the days our kids arrived, and the first time we sat down to dinner in our own place. I'd remember the way her lips felt and her body. And I knew, sitting there in that hospital room and watching her face, that all the bad would be forgotten and I'd keep re-membering only the good.

I felt about as vulnerable at that moment, Norman, as I have *ever* felt. And as much without control. I despised both feelings, I despised my helplessness, my wanting her that badly, my needing her.

"For God's sake, please don't go and die on me," I whispered to her. "I *need* you."

So I had at last said it aloud, and the heavens hadn't opened. But she'd had to be unconscious before I was able to blast the words past my teeth.

So what was the good? She hadn't heard me. She

didn't know. Yet I felt she *should* know even without my telling her. Hadn't I chosen her, asked her to spend her life with me? Couldn't she just look at me and *know* how much I loved and needed her? Looking at me, she must have gotten a totally different picture of what I felt. Otherwise, she wouldn't have started acting towards me as she did. It would have been too irrational.

Freud once described love as an irrational phenomenon. He said that the entire process of falling in love verges on the abnormal, and that anyone falling in love suffers from a compulsiveness and from a blindness to reality. All of which I once accepted as springing directly from the mouth of God and treated my patients accordingly, as did other of our Freud-oriented psychotherapists. The result was that we sometimes managed to effectively cure the alleged abnormalities of the very ones who stood out among us as *not* being abnormal and as *not* needing a cure.

What I'd say now, Norman, is that, in the midst of all the turmoil and pain and debasing foolishness we have to push our way through, if we're lucky enough to find one other person we truly feel something for, then all the rest of it doesn't matter. Without this feeling, we face little more than a long slide down a garbage chute. And for the Freudians to so cavalierly describe this single saving grace as an irrational phenomenon, for them to dismiss its blessings and mock its small blemishes in such arrogant terms, is potentially destructive and morally obscene.

If I'm coming across a bit shrill on this, Norman, it's because I'm really angry about it. Whatever good

Freud's theories have managed to bring about in other areas—and I'd be the first to admit it's considerable—he seems to have dug a snakepit for us in the garden of love. But I'm not trying to blame Freud for *all* my troubles with Barbara. I do accept my own full share of that.

What I'm finally reduced to is my occasional fantasizing, my trying to imagine what I might do differently, given another chance. And there are some things I like to imagine Barbara doing differently too. If it ever came down to it, I think I might be happy to settle for just one. I think I'd have just wanted her to be able to know—even without my ever speaking of it or saying a word—simply from *looking* at me, how much I really loved and needed her.

October 19

I'M GOING TO HAVE TO REALLY push myself today, Norman. I sensed it the minute I woke up this morning.
Before I even opened my eyes I knew it was there,
waiting for me, that nice warm cocoon of self-pity
that's getting to feel so good I just want to huddle
inside and never come out. I'm having to watch for it
more often lately. I've avoided talking about it because
this isn't supposed to be one of those damned journals
on dying. Still, it's there, and though I loathe it, I
can't say it's not.

I don't know how good I'm going to be at this. At
dying, I mean. The thing is, you just get one shot at
it and there's no real preparing. Some say you're

preparing in one way or another all your life, but that's just a lot of crap. When it comes down to it, it's all surprises—and none of them any good. Even for me, a doctor. There's still more fear, more awe, and more pain than I expected. I shouldn't bitch about the pain. It's manageable There are so many worse types of cancer available. But I'll tell you this, Norman: relative pain levels are a hell of a lot different when you're experiencing them yourself than when you're reading about them in some medical text. What you have to do, mostly, is think about other things. Which isn't always easy, but is one of the reasons I have these tapes going. Talking to you is supposed to help get me through this in reasonably decent shape. But I'll be damned if I feel much like talking about love this morning.

Still, that's exactly what I'm going to do.

That sounds noble and righteous, but it's all just a pose, a lot of last-minute posturing. I'm just playing to the gallery, and it's so utterly characteristic it's almost funny. I've always needed some sort of audience and I've always responded to it, even in tennis. Remember, Norman? I could be flat on my ass and down five love, until someone walked over to watch. Then I'd start tearing up the court like a teen-aged maniac. And if my audience turned out to be an attractive female, I'd go altogether crazy. How is that for a statement on my emotional growth? Past forty and I still had to do handsprings to impress the girls.

I guess my problem, Norman, if you want to call it a problem, was that I absolutely refused to be considered out of contention. In *anything*. I always had to feel I was in there, with a chance to cop the prize. And that applied especially to women, although I was never what you'd call a chaser. I never felt compelled to bed down with every attractive female I saw. But neither did I want any attractive woman to ever look at me and not feel, somewhere deep in the hindquarters of her fancy, that here was a man she might just possibly enjoy knowing and loving.

But what disturbs me most professionally, is the thought of all those who came to me for help with their love traumas, and whom I believed I was helping, but whom I may have actually betrayed because I was so unquestioning a disciple of Freud. If I had only done a little more thinking of my own in this area, the one in which our entire therapeutic structure is probably most shaky, I might have helped my patients more and hurt them less. And this applies particularly to that wildly flowering subdivision of love we call "infidelity." Because if there's going to be real trouble in any male-female relationship, a large part of it starts or ends up squarely in the middle of this section. Lack of fidelity is the tempting poisoned apple we're constantly biting into, and it's never out of season. And whether or not we happen to be nibbling away at it ourselves at any given moment, we always seem to get a perverse sort of pleasure from talking about it.

I think if a poll were ever taken to determine the all-time, most popular discussion topic among married people, infidelity would be the overwhelming first choice. In living rooms, kitchens, and bedrooms, in lecture halls and auditoriums, in study groups and

TV panels, the subject of marital infidelity is talked, argued, analyzed, and dissected into tiny pieces. Why? Freud would of course credit it to his theory that all men wanted to sexually conquer all women and that all women probably wanted them to. But this concept holds about as much true logic for a thinking psychotherapist as the doctrine of original sin holds for a priest. It's fine as long as you don't have to prove it.

Nevertheless, we're hardly monogamous by nature. There does have to be more than just one possible mate for each of us. It's nature's insurance for the perpetuation of the species. No matter how much in love we may be with one member of the opposite sex, we're not automatically immune to the appeal of all other members of the opposite sex. So we often think about that fact, we sometimes do something about it, and we almost always talk about it.

Academically stated on that basis, the whole subject of infidelity comes across as quite simple and logical. But that's only in words. Translated into action, reaction, passion, and pain, it ends up confused, complex, and utterly without logic. Families are broken, children are maimed, psyches are twisted, and general disaster is left in its wake. Yet, curiously, it's not our acts of infidelity in themselves that cause most of the trouble. It's our response to them. And the way most of us have been conditioned to respond makes about as much sense as a knee-jerk reflex.

What do we want from one another, Norman? I'm supposed to know. I was *trained* to know. And I once thought I did know. Now I'm just not sure. What we're supposed to want, of course, is love. Yet we have some very strange ways of going about getting it. We accuse. We threaten. We hurt. We punish. We retaliate. As if such things would somehow generate more love than the offering of love itself. In our panic, in our fear of losing love, we do everything possible to ensure its loss. And just in case there's a chance we may not be losing it quickly and thoroughly enough by ourselves, we sometimes hire professional experts to help us lose it. And in more cases than I enjoy remembering, Norman, the expert in question turned out to be me.

Let me tell you about a gentle, lovely, and sadly innocent woman who happened to be one of them.

Her name was Henrietta and she had a very nice life going for her. She had a considerate and loving husband, a couple of healthy kids, a comfortable home, and no money worries. But unfortunately, she also had a friend, who was honest, forthright, moral and had a strong sense of justice.

One day the friend felt compelled to tell Henrietta that her husband, Tommy, had been fooling around with a cute little piece of fluff from his office. Naturally it was for Henrietta's own good that she told her. She felt she owed it to her as a friend.

Henrietta didn't believe it at first. Impossible! She was that naive about the whole thing. But her friend persisted, brought irrefutable proof, and at last convinced Henrietta that it was indeed possible. And with that, Henrietta's whole world collapsed. Unable to orient herself to the violent new tilt in her horizon, she came to me for help. And who recommended me? Her friend, of course.

"What should I do, Doctor?" Henrietta asked me.

"What do you *want* to do?" I asked back.

We call that self-interpretation, Norman. It's supposed to help the patient to help himself in understanding his problem. Sometimes it works and sometimes it doesn't. With Henrietta, it didn't. All she wanted to do was wish everything back the way it had been before. But she couldn't. So we had to go on from there.

So far, she hadn't told Tommy she knew about the other woman. She was afraid. Still loving and wanting her husband, she didn't want to push either of them into taking any kind of precipitous action.

But her most severe problem when she came to me was her own self-doubt. Her initial reaction to Tommy's infidelity was to blame herself. She believed that if she had been everything a good, proper, and attractive wife was supposed to be, as she thought she *had* been, there would have been no need for Tommy to look elsewhere to satisfy his desires. And if his desires were sexual, then she had surely failed him sexually, either through her lack of appeal in that area or her lack of ability.

And what was I doing to help her during this period? Well for one thing, I was listening, which in itself is a form of therapy. But mostly, I was trying to get her to stop blaming herself. This was the main focus of my treatment. Understand, Norman. Henrietta wasn't an especially brilliant or worldly woman.

She was reasonably intelligent in most things, but naive when it came to the complexities of the male-female relationship. Like most of the middle-class married women I've known or treated over the years, she believed that if she fulfilled her wifely duties in the bedroom without stint or reservation, her husband would have no need to be unfaithful.

So to get rid of Henrietta's unreasonable guilt and self-doubt, I began her education on the subject of marital infidelity. I let her know that as far as Tommy's faithlessness was concerned, it probably had nothing at all to do with her, the way she looked, or what she may have done. If her Tommy had this need to get off a few random shots with some hot, wiggly young thing on Thursday afternoons, he would have had the same need regardless of what may have been waiting for him at home. I also gave her the full text on man's not being a monogamous animal by nature and his being therefore vulnerable to all sorts of sexual temptation. It was pretty much my standard, fifty-dollar-an-hour infidelity treatment, but I think I did an exceptionally good job of it with Henrietta. I liked her, I felt sorry for her, and I genuinely wanted to help her. She was innocent, she was a victim, and she was hurting.

It required about six or seven months of concentrated therapy, but by the end of that time Henrietta was no longer innocent or blaming herself for Tommy's infidelity. She was in the midst of a blazing love affair of her own. She was liberated. Not only had I wakened her to the fact that man wasn't monogamous by nature, but that woman wasn't either.

There was suddenly a whole new world out there for her, and she had started reaching for her own share of it.

All of which might have been fine for some women, but it wasn't fine for Henrietta. She simply couldn't handle an involvement with more than one man at a time. There are certain, basic, minimum amounts of deceit required for successful marital infidelity. For one thing, you have to be able to lie and do it quickly, imaginatively, and convincingly. For another, you have to be able to compartmentalize your thoughts and emotions. It's important that they don't overlap or become confused during moments of extreme passion or tenderness. Also, you have to be intellectually capable of accepting the fundamental philosophy of all successful, long-term, extra-marital lovers—to believe you can love and be loyal to one member of the opposite sex at the same time you are loving and being loyal to other members of that sex. And finally, and perhaps most importantly, you have to be able to remain free of disrupting guilt.

I don't mean to be facetious about this, Norman. I'm suddenly aware that it may sound a bit that way, but I'm quite serious about what I've said. And I've had enough intimate, professional knowledge of extra-marital love affairs over the years to know what I'm talking about. The real survivors at this business do qualify on each of the checkpoints I mentioned. I've known men and women who have carried on beautiful love affairs for as long as twenty-five years, while each of the partners has been happily married to someone else. And some of the marriages have actually been helped by what was taking place outside them. The continuing love affairs not only served as safety valves during stressful periods at home, but also provided a secret sense of gratitude to the husband or wife who so unknowingly was making the whole thing possible.

But Henrietta possessed absolutely none of the requirements. She was practically manic when it came to lying. She'd had a strict Sunday-school upbringing and kept imagining her tongue getting black and her nose growing longer. She was also incapable of dividing her loyalty or of compartmentalizing her thoughts and emotions. The whole thing confused her to the point where she was so fearful of calling out the wrong name at the wrong time, that she all but paralyzed herself sexually.

By this time, however, Henrietta was no longer being treated by me. She had dismissed herself from my care shortly after I completed her education, removed her self-doubt about Tommy's infidelity, and inadvertently launched her on some reciprocal infidelity of her own. That's one of the major hazards of the shrink business, Norman. Patients can dismiss themselves from treatment at will and there's nothing we're able to do about it. Sometimes it works out all right. Sometimes when they *feel* they're ready to break away, they *are* ready. Other times, they're not. In Henrietta's case, it was like having her walk out of an operating room with her surgery only half completed.

The thing was, I had taught her a new way to look at herself as well as at the whole male-female relationship, but I hadn't yet taught her how to *deal* effectively with either one. I had dumped Henrietta into the complex, sophisticated world of infidelity like a contemporary Alice-in-Wonderland and that was exactly how she responded to it—wide-eyed and filled with wonder. She also responded to it as the woman she still was under the thin veneer of worldliness I had pasted over her. So that when she did let herself fall in love with another man, she did it in the only way she could—completely and honestly. And on that basis, she couldn't see herself continuing to live with her husband. So she packed up her kids, moved out, and got a divorce. Which pretty much broke up her Tommy, who still loved and wanted her and had no idea that his little harmless playing around was about to explode like a time bomb and blow his home and family sky-high.

As for Henrietta's new love, well, I'm afraid that once she and her kids were on his doorstep, he didn't want them. Which happens more often than not.

So Henrietta and her two kids were left floating in that sad limbo that lies somewhere between the old lives the divorced have left behind and the new ones they hope to get. And the getting is rarely easy. By the time Henrietta came back to me for further therapy and reported all this, she had been trying to get herself a new life for almost three years, while she and her kids grew that much older and more confused and her Tommy married the little piece of fluff from his office out of spite, pique, and an apparently latent urge to self-destruction.

Now isn't that a story, Norman? My God, I'm full

of stories. I'm beginning to sound like a soap opera. Except that unfortunately, all my stories are true and not the product of some scriptwriter. And just as unfortunately, I seem to be playing the heavy in most of them. I was certainly the heavy in this last one. Given another chance to help her today, I'd do things differently. I'd listen to her less, I'd ask her less for self-interpretation, and I'd tell her a whole lot more.

Which was why she came to me in the first place. She didn't come to me to be educated. She didn't come to me to be enlightened as to the true nature of the male-female relationship. And she certainly didn't come to me to be made over into the sexual sophisticate she wasn't. She came to me for only one reason—for advice on how to save her marriage. And I didn't give it to her. I was too busy being a superior-type shrink and twaddling around with superior psychotherapeutic procedures to give her the simple, practical advice she so desperately needed. All I had to do was get her to sit down with her Tommy and tell him she loved him and that she knew he loved her, but that she also knew he was fooling around and wanted him to stop because she couldn't cope with it. And do you know something, Norman? The guy would have done it. He would have been so scared of losing her and the kids that he would have stopped. At least for a while. And the next time, if he did try it again, he'd probably be more careful and maybe not get caught. But in the meantime, they'd be living together and loving each other and sharing their kids and not blowing everything all to hell for no worthwhile reason.

The truth of it is, Norman, from where I'm sitting now I don't really consider infidelity an automatically worthwhile reason to break up an otherwise decent marriage. When I was younger, I did. When I was younger, I was foolish enough to believe that was one transgression you didn't get away with and didn't forgive and didn't deserve to have forgiven. Infidelity didn't just mean the end of love, it meant the end of the world. I was that certain of myself, of my wife, and of the ultimate perfection of a true and proper love.

I no longer feel that way. I'm obviously less certain of myself and of my wife. And so far as a true and proper love is concerned, any such image of perfection is no more than a state of mind. And a very temporary one at that. What's perfect today, could be less perfect tomorrow. And by the day after tomorrow, who knows? In the meantime, as long as love is there, I wouldn't question it.

Henrietta had two pieces of very bad luck. The first was that she had an honest, forthright, and moral friend. And the second was that she came to me for help. I helped her right out of a husband she loved, and a marriage she wanted, into God only knows what.

She dropped out of therapy again after about six months and I lost track of her. Thinking of her, I hope she and her kids are all right. I hope she found someone new to love and to believe in as she once loved and believed in her Tommy.

But I'm sure she hasn't.

October 20

WHEN MY SON, DAVID, WAS very young, Norman—I think he was either in kindergarten or the first grade at the time—I once taught him an important lesson in love and character building, although neither of us understood it then.

We lived close enough to his school in those days for him to walk there, which he usually did, unless it happened to be raining. Then either my wife or I would drive him. He wasn't a lazy kid and he actually enjoyed the walking. It made him feel grown up and independent. He certainly never objected or complained about it. But one sunny spring morning, he suddenly decided he didn't feel like walking that day.

He wanted to be driven. When I asked him why he couldn't walk on such a beautiful morning, he wouldn't tell me. Or else he couldn't. Maybe he had no reason at all. Maybe he just felt like having me drive him that morning. Or maybe something or someone had frightened him the day before. There could have been any number of reasons. Or none. It didn't matter. He wanted to be driven, and he absolutely refused to budge out of the house unless he was.

It was the kind of thing that Barbara would have normally handled, but she was off volunteering at the local hospital that day, so I was stuck with it. One of the disadvantages of having an office at home is that you're around the house too much. And because you're there, you're subject to this kind of crisis when your thoughts and concerns are wholly involved with the day's work. On this particular morning, I was expecting an early patient and needed time to go over some notes. In any case, I was in no mood for my son's nonsense. Let him pick some other morning to act up. I hadn't the time to fool with his temperament today.

So I told him there was no reason for him to be driven on such a lovely day, and that he'd better get going or he'd be late. He cried louder. I got angrier. Not only at him, but also at my absent wife. What right had she to be off volunteering—off emptying a bunch of goddamned bedpans and leaving me stuck with this? Damn it! I had a patient coming any minute.

I calmed down and used logic and applied psychology. I explained to my son that we all had our duties and obligations. Mommy's was to take care of the house and cook and things like that. Mine was to take care of my patients. And his was to walk to school on nice mornings and get an education. And unless we were sick or had some other good reason not to do these things, we *did* them, by God! This was how we developed as human beings. This was how we made our lives productive and worthwhile. Sometimes Mommy and Daddy didn't much feel like doing what they had to do either, but they still did it. David must learn to do it also. He was just a little boy, of course, but the principle was the same at any age. You fulfilled your obligations.

It was no use. My son had no ears for my logic and applied psychology. Something deep inside him had closed and my words were locked out. He wanted to be driven to school that morning and that was that. Seeing how it was, I moved on to the next step in his character building. I grabbed his little hand with my big one and dragged him, kicking, screaming, and crying, out the front door. "Now go to school!" I commanded and went back into the house and into my office to get on with my work.

Except that I didn't get on with my work immediately, Norman. First, I looked out the window. And there he was, my son, trudging forlornly up the road, this tiny, solitary, broken, weeping figure, with its golden blond hair on top and its little matchstick legs on the bottom, slowly losing itself in the distance. And this was my logic, my applied psychology.

And I thought, Oh, my God, and started to weep myself.

My own father, who had little of my technical knowledge of such things and nothing of my experience and background, would have handled the whole crisis very differently. And the only thing he would have used to guide him would have been love. If I had insanely insisted one day that I wanted him to carry me to school on his shoulders, and if he saw that crazy as it seemed it was somehow desperately important to me, he would have shrugged, kissed me, and carried me to school on his shoulders. He would have let my character development take care of itself. Or else he would have postponed it until a time when I might have been better able to cope with it.

But then, unlike me, my father didn't have the problems of a lot of seriously ill patients to worry about.

That was another excuse I often used: the demands and pressures of my work. And that's fairly typical of most of us in the medical profession, Norman. Everyone has their own work, of course, but surely a doctor's work is more vital, more absorbing, more all-encompassing than anyone else's. We've taught the layman to believe this, and we believe it ourselves. Or if we don't truly believe it, we at least pretend we do because it excuses a multitude of sins. Foremost among which is that abysmal self-absorption, that utter selfishness that allows us to neglect, shut out, and hurt those closest to us under the guise of humanitarianism and professional dedication.

Even now, I suspect my motives on that sunny spring morning with my son. The thing is, Norman, how much was I truly concerned about developing his character, and how much was I thinking about the amount of time I would have had to waste driving him to school when I had work waiting in my office? Which was more important to me, my work or my son? With a child's instinctive wisdom, my son may even have been testing me, testing his daddy's love against his constant competitor—his daddy's work. If it was indeed a test of my love, a test of me as a devoted father, I failed it badly that day.

I also failed it at other times.

My son was a thumbsucker, Norman, and do you know what that was for me? That was a bloody earthquake! I mean, for a shrink's kid to walk around with his goddamn thumb in his mouth was hardly the greatest advertisement in the world for his old man's professional competence.

I often joked about it, but it was strictly gallows humor. I didn't really find it amusing. When David's thumb was in his mouth, it used to hurt me just to look at him. I was ashamed of the way I felt, but I couldn't help it. The thumb bothered the hell out of me. And the fact that I *was* bothered hurt me even more. It also hurt my son, although I did my best to cover it. It's hard to fool children about basic feelings. They have the fine, mystic instincts of certain small animals. They depend on them for survival. My son knew his thumb was one sure way to reach me and he used it. But he was very subtle. He might remove his thumb from his mouth as soon as I came into a room, but never soon enough to keep me from seeing where it had been.

But I think what bothers me most, Norman, is that I can't seem to remember taking pleasure in him the

way other fathers take pleasure in their kids, the way
my father took pleasure in me. I mean active, conscious pleasure, totally absorbed pleasure. Even when
I played with him, it was practically ritualistic. It was
little more than a duty I felt compelled to perform
because this was what good fathers were supposed to
do with their sons. It was never a spontaneous thing
for me. I was never wholly with him, never wholly
without thoughts of other things. And I'm sure my
son knew that too. But whatever small scraps of attention I was willing to toss him, he was eager to take.
In fact he always insisted on collecting what he had
come to understand was due him from me in the way
of playtime, whether it was the regular after-dinner
play period, or the Sunday morning ritual. "Daddy,"
he would say, "it's time to play with me now." And
that was even before he was old enough to tell time.

Still, there was one little game we played together
when he was about three or four years old that I did
kind of enjoy—even though it was really a terrible
game for a shrink to be playing with his kid. My
God, it was all about cowboys and overt violence that
involved toy six-shooters and our pretending to shoot
at one another from behind different pieces of living-
room furniture. Terrible, terrible. I could have been
drummed out of the Shrink Club if anyone had seen
and reported it. But at least it allowed my son to get
rid of his hostilities by shooting me dead every night
after dinner. Because according to the script, I invariably lost the final shootout and ended up sprawled
flat on the carpet, eyes closed and arms flung wide,

while David softly sang "Bury Me Not on the Lone Prairie" for my last rites.

Then, since I enjoyed getting kissed by my son, and his kisses were normally scarce, I managed to work a few out of him as part of my regular resurrection. The only way I would come back from the dead was by his kissing me. Which he did faithfully and which didn't seem too unreasonable to him since he already knew about Sleeping Beauty being wakened by a kiss from the Prince. He didn't yet know about death, of course. It was just another kind of sleep, in which you simply lay with your eyes closed until something or someone woke you. And in our game, it was up to him to take care of the waking.

But one evening my son decided to see what would happen if he let me stay dead. He had just finished singing the ritual lament and there I was, flat out with my eyes closed, waiting for my resurrection kiss. When it didn't come on schedule, I peeked out from under one lid and saw my son gravely considering me. Then he slowly got up and backed out of the room, watching me as he went. I continued to lie there, unmoving. After a few minutes he came back and watched me some more from the doorway. His round, pink face was serious under his cowboy hat. Important decisions were being weighed. He still held his six-shooter in one hand, but the thumb from the other hand was in his mouth. Then, having made his decision, he came back and resurrected me with his kiss.

Apparently even a part-time father was better than none.

I'm sure there were times later, especially when he felt I had let him down in some way, that he regretted not having left me flat out on the carpet that day. And of course I did let him down, if not always by what I did, then surely by what I didn't do. And what I didn't do most frequently was simply to accept and love him without question, without judgment, and without thinking about it. Damn it, Norman! That kid was my *son*, not my patient. And I wasn't his doctor. I was his father. But I didn't always treat him that way. I surely didn't treat him the way my father treated me. I never had the slightest doubt about how much my father loved me, Norman. Whatever I did, right or wrong, I always felt my father would back me. Against the whole damn world, if necessary. My son never felt that. He had no reason to feel it.

When he was about ten, David was dragged home by the collar one Sunday morning by a man who claimed that he and some other boys had been throwing snowballs at his house and that David had broken a window. My son denied it. He said he had been there but hadn't thrown any snowballs. The man said David was lying. My son shouted that it was the man himself who was the goddamn liar, and who was I going to believe anyway, this dirty, mean old bastard or my own son? And of course I came through beautifully by not only believing the dirty, mean old bastard, but by writing him a check for the window repair and chastising my son for swearing and for engaging in malicious mischief.

In the house, David really tore into me. Losing

control, he screamed that I didn't love him, that I
didn't care anything about him at all. He said that if
he were my *real* son and not just my adopted son, I
wouldn't have acted that way. He also said he hated
me and intended to run away and look for his real
father the first chance he got. He really threw it at
me that day, the whole collection of separate little
nightmares that haunt all adoptive parents.

Again, I find myself thinking of my own father
and how differently he would have also handled this
one. And how simply. What he would have done was
stick his jaw two inches from the man's face, tell him
that if his son said he didn't break any window then,
by God, he didn't break any window, and if the man
wanted to make anything more out of it he could
goddamn well try right now. But of course my father
was an essentially simple, even a crude man. He didn't
understand any of the niceties, any of the more subtle
aspects of human relations. He didn't even know anything about fair, unbiased judgments where those he
loved were concerned. He would have said, "*What*
fair? *What* unbiased? Am I a Supreme Court judge?
My own are my own. Let the judges worry about
being fair and unbiased."

Not only the judges, Norman, but also the shrinks.
We're so fair and unbiased, it's disgusting. And we
dispense these qualities like vending machines. Slip us
our fifty bucks for a forty-five-minute hour, press the
right buttons, and out come all our fair, unbiased bits
of advice on human behavior. We have whole lists.
We even have a special list for your children, with
special child-oriented axioms. We tell you to avoid

feeling sorry for your kids because it may cloud your judgment. We warn you not to let them impress you with their assumed weaknesses or you may turn them into parasites. We preach about the fallacy of following your first impulses in reacting to their problems, instead of carefully weighing the steps to be taken. We caution you to take time to specifically train them in their interpersonal relationships and advise you to always try to set good examples for them by your own behavior. And if you want a few dozen more of these little homilies to help turn your kids into well-adjusted citizens of the world, just keep slipping your fifty-dollar bills into our hungry slots and we'll keep them popping out.

But what we don't tell you is that if you love your kids and let them know you love them, that if you're steadily loyal and don't let them feel you're sitting in constant judgment, making them earn your love over and over again, minute by minute, then you can pretty much forget the rest of it because you don't need it and it all becomes just a lot of pretentious and confusing crap.

Still, maybe I'm being a bit hard on myself for that snowball incident with my son. It wasn't nearly as clear-cut as I may have made it seem. David did have a fair history of chronic lying behind him. He also had an even greater history of exactly the kind of mischief for which he stood accused that morning. My son was no sweet little innocent. And of course I wasn't about to let myself be conned either. So my judgment on that day wasn't only fair and unbiased, it was absolutely reasonable. Or was I also expected to suspend reason for the sake of loyalty and love? No, that would have been just too ridiculous.

Then how come it turned out that my son was proven innocent that Sunday morning, that he had been telling the truth all along while that other son-ofabitch had been lying through his teeth?

Isn't that lovely, Norman? So how are we supposed to learn? And even when we do learn, why does it always seem to happen too late?

In this particular case, one of my son's friends demonstrated more loyalty and love for him than I did. When he found out that David had been stuck with the rap, he came to me and confessed to having broken the window himself. He said David had indeed just been watching that morning and hadn't done a thing. He said he wanted me to know this because David felt so bad about my not believing him. I thanked the boy and told him he was a good and honorable friend.

Naturally, I apologized to my son. But I doubt that it meant very much. By his estimate, I had failed him. I had shown neither trust nor love. It did little good to point out that his record in the areas in which he had been accused wasn't the greatest, and that although my mistake was an unhappy one, it wasn't really too unreasonable. He didn't want to know about that. He didn't want to hear anything about all the times he *had* lied to me. Not that I blamed him—he held a good, strong tactical position and was smart to want to make the most of it. But, apart from the role-playing, the basics remained unchanged. David *did* consider himself grievously wronged, grievously abandoned by me. He *did* consider himself unloved. He *did* believe that if he were my natural and not my adopted son, I would have behaved differently. And for all practical purposes, if you believe such things to be so, you can't help but be affected as if they *were* so.

I've been learning about adoption over the years, Norman. I told you at the start of these tapes how I felt about it, and I meant every word. I'm sure my son would never have doubted my love if he hadn't been told he was adopted, if he hadn't felt different from other kids right from the start, if he hadn't felt constantly compelled to dig for proof of my love because he *was* different. Maybe I haven't been the world's most perfect father, but who has? There's obviously no such thing. Nor are there any fine lines drawn between the good fathers and the bad ones. There are only fathers who can make their kids feel loved and those who can't. Evidently I was one of those who couldn't.

Which is about as sad a thing as I can think of to say. I mean sad for my son. He was the one who was cheated, who was made to feel abandoned and alone when there was no true need for him to feel that way. Because I did love him, and I do now.

One summer night I sat with him during a thunderstorm. He was badly frightened. He didn't say he was frightened. He wouldn't. Not ever. But I could feel him shaking. I talked to him, probably not making much sense, but just trying to make little human noises in the darkness. And I held his hand. Normally, he wouldn't have put up with such a thing, but he let me do it this time. And we sat there together, the two of us.

And that was about all there was to it. Yet for years afterward, my son would keep remembering it. He would keep bringing it up and talking about it.

He would say, kind of wistfully, "Remember how we sat together during that storm, Daddy?"

And I'd say, "I sure do. That was some storm."

"I thought the thunder would never stop," he'd tell me.

"It was bad, all right," I'd agree.

"But still..." he would say, groping a little and not quite understanding it, "there was something sort of nice about it."

And he was right. I guess there just weren't enough thunderstorms. For us both.

October 21

___

How leisurely i die, Norman. Sometimes I have the feeling the whole thing is taking place in a kind of slow-motion haze, almost like one of those arty, misty-lensed film sequences that are so popular with movie directors these days. And during those times when I can truly accept the fact of it, it's not really too bad.

Do you know what's happening to me now? I'm going off somewhere surrounded by my own special conspiracy of silence. I know I've done this to myself, shut myself off deliberately, but that makes it no easier. I seem to hear no words, no sounds with any meaning anymore. And do you know what sound I think I miss most? The sound of a tennis ball meeting gut. I think, of all the sounds I've loved in the course of my remarkably short and unvaried life, that was my favorite. I've liked the happy pop of corks leaving bottles and the whirring of hand mowers being pushed through grass, which you don't get to hear anymore anyway. There's just the fracturing sound of those damn gasoline engines on Sunday mornings now. But nothing could quite match that soft melodic note of a fuzzy ball meeting a racket's sweet spot.

Tennis could sure frustrate the hell out of me, Norman, and no one knows that better than you. But when it was right, few things could give me as much pleasure. I don't think I ever took it for granted either. Since I hit thirty, I don't think I've ever walked onto a tennis court without actively feeling grateful for just being able to be there with a racket in my hand, to move, and to feel the sun. I guess I've always been a pretty physical kind of guy. I've even been rather vain about my body, which makes it all the harder to watch what's beginning to happen to it now.

Yet, that's really pretty juvenile, isn't it? I know I was once dust and soon will be again, so why should my body matter? At best, it's just rented. It hangs in time like an empty suit in a closet. To take pride in such a thing is more than stupid. It's obscene. Where's my philosophy, my religion, my awareness of infinity and my place in it? Where are all the things that are supposed to make dying easier?

So far, they're not here. And increasingly, Norman, I think I'm getting a little afraid I might need them.

A while back, when I first heard the news, the

prognosis, there were moments when I thought about handling it my own way and setting my own timetable. I figured it would at least give me some control. But I've stopped thinking that way. For one thing, these tapes have given me a definite, almost pleasant sense of purpose. And for another, I just don't feel it's my style. Besides, there's no point in adding to the embarrassing suicide rate among psychiatrists. I once saw the statistics and they were incredible. I don't remember the exact figures, but I think the incidence of suicide among practicing shrinks was somewhere around three times that of the population in general. And that's sure as hell trying to tell us *something*. Either about the kind of miserable character who is drawn to this kind of work, or about the nature of the work itself, or both.

The fact is, we don't have any real answers to that. All we have are little jokes. We say we have to be a bit nuts ourselves to want to spend so much time with nuts. We say sick is beautiful, man; well is square. Things like that. But not all the jokes are without their little nibbling teeth of truth. And when it comes right down to the idea of suicide itself, few of us feel much like laughing. I don't mean we walk around brooding about killing ourselves. What I mean is, few of us are ever free of possible suicidals among our patients. And even fewer of us are without the memory of patients who actually did take their own lives.

Of all the frustrations, of all the traumas we suffer as occupational hazards, that one is by far the worst. You feel so useless, so damn futile when it happens.

The thing clogs your brain. You walk around wondering what you might have missed seeing. You plague yourself thinking about what you might have done differently. You go back searching for things you might have done wrong. But you're never really going to know. Nor are you ever going to get the chance to do it better. Not with that one, anyway, not with the one you've just lost. And you soon learn it's not going to help you much with the next one either. Because they're all different.

When I'm really down, Norman, when I'm really feeling depressed and self-destructive, all I have to do is recite my list of suicides and beat my breast like an old Jew on the Day of Atonement. I don't know whether my list is longer or shorter than those of other psychiatrists. I've never compared it with anyone else's. Remember Sheila Miller, the woman who turned on the gas and managed to blow up her house and kids along with herself? That was about as bad as they come. Except that Sheila was an *ex*-patient when it happened. I hadn't seen her in more than a year. There are others on my list whom I was actually treating at the time they made their moves. So if it's possible for such things to be worse for you as their doctor, as their alleged savior, these were worse. And high among those in this group was Patty Litchuk.

Patty was young, early twenties, I guess, pretty, bright, one of that great army of young women that emigrates from towns to cities each year to enrich their lives and fill the clerical needs of our large corporations. Patty had been raised as a devout Catholic, parochial education and all, but had stopped practicing her religion entirely by the time she came to me as a patient. Which was one of the major reasons she needed help. The church can be a great, warm, all-embracing mother to those raised within its folds. Its disciplines are strong and supportive. When mother is suddenly no longer there, the resulting vacuum can be troubling and confusing—even dangerous. And it proved so for Patty.

It was her new sexual freedom, her new and different standards of morality that were giving her the most trouble. In love with a dazzlingly eligible young executive at the company where she worked, she had managed to accept the idea of living with him out of wedlock but was having difficulty coping with some of the fringe demands that her new and sinful life-style were making upon her. Because, regardless of what her lover was telling her, and in spite of what she was telling herself, the good Catholic psyche with which she had lived for so many years wasn't fully convinced. It still made her feel guilty and sinful as hell.

But what finally drove Patty to seek psychiatric help was the nature of the man himself and some of the things he was asking her to do. He had apparently been on the big-city singles scene for a long time and was a real swinger. One of the first problems Patty came to me with involved his evident passion for hardcore pornography. He enjoyed having her share some of the really raunchy sex shows and movies with him and she just couldn't stomach that kind of thing. It sickened her. But even more importantly, she considered it evil, ugly, and obscene. What troubled her most, when she came to me, was not knowing whether she was right or wrong in the way she felt about it.

I quickly let her know it wasn't a question of right or wrong. I told her different people reacted to such things in different ways. Some found it sexually stimulating, others found it amusing or just plain dull, and still others—like herself—were simply turned off and revolted by it. Everyone reacted out of their own particular backgrounds and tastes. And since she had been raised within the strict, morally and sexually inhibiting guidelines of the church, it wasn't at all surprising for her to be reacting in the way she was.

But didn't I think, she insisted, that such things were evil and ugly no matter *what* your background? No, I told her. I didn't think that at all. And I also told her the word *evil* was a dangerous word to fool with. It had an unhappy history. Too many cruel and restrictive abuses had been committed by those who assigned themselves the responsibility for stamping it out. As for something being what she called dirty? Well, I said, that, like beauty, was pretty much in the eye of the beholder.

So by not confirming her feelings of wrongdoing, Norman, I did manage to give her a kind of negative reassurance. She still may not have been comfortable watching some of those sex circuses, but she was at least able to tolerate them under pressure from her raunchy beloved without feeling herself condemned to the first circle of hell.

But voyeurism soon turned out to be only the tip

of the iceberg. The guy was a true sexual adventurer, with an incredible imagination in bed and an appetite to match. And he apparently got an extra charge out of Patty's background of religious inhibition and comparative innocence. There *are* such men, Norman. When they've been playing around long enough, the excitement begins to pall. They have to come up with a unique approach every now and then. And little dark-haired Patty, coming to her Irwin full of love, virginity, and newly quiescent Catholicism, was clearly his unique approach of that year.

And Patty was madly in love. Apart from Irwin's farout sexuality, he was all her dreams come true. He was handsome, charming, worldly, and attentive— everything she had ever wanted in a man. Whatever would please him, whatever he asked in the way of sex or anything else, Patty was willing to grant. Also, once I had provided her with the needed assurance that none of this stuff was truly evil, it all became a lot easier for her to accept. In a sense, I had become her father confessor. Her regular visits to my office had replaced her earlier visits to the confessional. But I was better than a priest. I granted her absolution without even requiring penance. Just my regular fee.

So Patty was making good progress in coming to terms with her new lifestyle. Her anxieties had eased and were under control, and the disturbing memories of her religious upbringing, with its gnawing strictures, were pushed even further into the background. Irwin increased his demands. Starting with a *ménage à trois* and other kinds of group sex, the homo- and heterosexual orgies that followed represented pretty much the ultimate departure from Patty's, or for that matter anyone else's, point of origin. Yet Patty was so well indoctrinated by now in the boundless possibilities of sex as a major sport, that she was able to report these latest activities to me less as a confession of sin, requiring absolution, than as exciting adventures in which she was playing a major role. She had pretty much come full circle for a girl who once couldn't even stand the sight of porno movies.

At this stage in her therapy, Patty no longer seemed to be confessing to me. I think she seemed more interested in trying to shock me. But in one way or another, I was still fulfilling my function as a therapist for her. I was there. She was able to talk to me as she was able to talk to no one else. And when she did occasionally feel some uncertainty, some small fluttering of doubt about one thing or another, my supportiveness was enough to reassure her. Once in a while I did try to give warning of possible trouble ahead, to point out the essential futility of chasing kicks and thrills to the exclusion of more substantial goals. But it wasn't my job to try to change her life. At least I didn't consider it so. If this was the life she had chosen and apparently wanted, for whatever her reasons, all I could hope to do was keep her reasonably free of anxiety and functioning as well as possible within its parameters.

Then came earthquake time. The guy finally grew bored and kicked Patty out. With nothing left for him to teach her or introduce her to in the way of exotic erotica, he lost interest. Now she was just like all the rest of the thrill seekers in his crowd. So he went out and got himself another wide-eyed, innocent young thing from the company secretarial pool to help him start the process all over again. And because he found Patty's continued presence at work annoying and faintly embarrassing, he had her fired from her job.

When Patty told me all this, I wasn't really too surprised. But I still felt as though someone had kicked me in the gut. I still wanted to go after that sonofabitch myself and strangle him. But that wouldn't have helped Patty, just me.

The poor kid went into such a decline, into so severe a state of depression, that she wouldn't even go out to look for another job. I saw her almost every day during that period. Her entire ego seemed to have disintegrated. She wasn't angry at Irwin. She didn't despise him. She didn't blame him for throwing her out. She just blamed and despised herself. She felt she deserved whatever had happened to her. All the guilt she had sublimated during the past months, all her childhood visions of sin and perdition broke loose, attacked, and overwhelmed her. She felt used, unclean, unworthy of further love. "My God," she wept to me, "the things I've done."

I tried to be supportive. I assured her she was no different from what she had ever been. I told her she was the same lovely, warm, desirable young woman she had been before she ever met this guy. Maybe she had gone through a pretty miserable time, but it was all over now and she had to get on with the business of living. At one point I seriously considered hospitalizing her. But then her attitude seemed to get better and I decided to wait and see what happened.

What happened, Norman, was that one day when I left her alone in my office for a moment to get something, Patty left also. Through the window—and my office was on the sixth floor.

I had to explain it all to the police and someone from the coroner's office. I also had to explain it to Patty's father, a tired-looking factory worker from some town in the Midwest, when he came to claim her body. He sat in my office that morning, a small man with a busted nose and the same hurt, confused eyes as his daughter's, and he wept. He couldn't understand any part of it. He couldn't understand why his daughter had been coming to me for treatment in the first place. She had always been such a happy little girl, he said. He took out his wallet and showed me pictures—Patty wearing her First Communion dress, in cap and gown for her graduation from high school. They were the same kind of pictures you see in the papers when someone has died an unusual or violent enough death to make them briefly newsworthy. Patty looked like a real little angel in the pictures. And her father was right—she also looked very happy.

I carried her with me, very heavily, for a long time. You don't shake off that kind of thing easily, Norman. It just mixes in with your blood and stays. Sometimes when you're lying awake in the night, you can feel the separate pieces. And they're sharp.

Where did I go wrong with her?

I have different answers to that question now than I had when it happened. And the answers are a lot more decisive—and angrier. Because I know I'm running out of time, I find I'm also running out of patience with some of our more pious attitudes and pronouncements on how we should handle these things. I should have treated Patty differently from the beginning, Norman. She came to me screaming for help, and all I threw her for lifelines were a bunch of vague generalities—psychological banalities. I have opinions, damn it! I had them *then*. Why didn't I offer them to her? Why didn't I batter her over her poor confused head with them if necessary?

Right then and there, I should have told her what I believed about pornography. She needed me to say, "Yes, Patty it *is* ugly and wrong. Yes, it *is* revolting. Yes, it *does* take all the loveliness out of the act of love and reduce it to the level of whorehouse plumbing." And what did I do instead? I weaseled around with all those worn out, pedantic clichés about it not being a question of right or wrong, and about different people reacting to it in different ways. What goddamn cowardice! What crap!

There's no way of knowing of course, but I think if I had hit her with some of that right at the start and confirmed and strengthened her own feelings, there might have been a chance of her not going any further with the rest of it. Understand, Norman, I'm not claiming this approach would have been right for everyone, or that all porn must be regarded as the grease on the slide to hell. I'm simply saying I think it would have been right for *Patty*, for someone with *her* religious background and upbringing, for someone in whom guilt would always be present, no matter how well sublimated, just waiting to bust loose with that first traumatic crack in the ego.

I agree that censorship had to go, of course. It's not the job of the courts to police our morals. But the deluge of smut that's been pouring out of our newsstands, bookstores, and theaters since most of the legal barriers were lowered is overwhelming. I've seen teen-age kids on dates coming out of those hardcore movie sewers. They giggle nervously. They can't quite look at one another. And what have they been staring at—along with about a thousand strangers—for the past hour and a half? A full-color image of a twenty-foot penis, a vagina that fills the screen like a great gaping wound, a vortex of naked bodies, crawling over to one another like a nest of hibernating snakes. And these are just a few of the images of love, of our human mating experience, that these young people are carrying out of the theater and tucking away in some dark, quiet corner of their psyches.

Yet we who deal professionally with the psyche, we who are most responsible for its well-being, somehow manage not to speak out against this pestilence. I never have, nor do I know of any other psychiatrist who has. In our current climate of sexual liberation, it would be too dangerous. We'd be accused of psychological regression, of trying to inhibit the free and natural expression of the libido. So there we are again, Norman—victims of that same reverse bigotry that caused some of our newly enlightened psychotherapists to recommend more frequent use of the word *fuck* to their patients and to relegate the word *love* to the dustbins of sentimentality and Victorianism. Yet how much better than that was I with Patty? I was so concerned about overstepping my professional bounds, I was so worried about countertransference, about forcing my own feelings down the throat of my patient, that I carefully avoided—no, that's too mild—*deliberately copped out* of telling her the very things that may have helped keep her alive.

I don't know whether she would have even listened to me. But at least I would have tried. And she did respect me. She did care what I thought. She did lean on me for support, so I might have had some real leverage.

She made me her surrogate priest and I thought I had granted her absolution. But I guess I simply lacked the faith and courage to have ever really offered her anything more than just the final sacrament.

October 23

IT'S BEEN A LONG TIME since my divorce, Norman, a few years, but my wife hasn't remarried yet. And I'm glad.

Oh, I suppose from time to time I've made a few of the usual obligatory jokes about feeding—or is it *beating*—a dead horse? I forget which. But they were just noises, a pose. I've never really minded the alimony. In fact I've rather enjoyed the payments. They were at least a tie, a link, a continuing sign of her dependence, even of her *need* for me. Which, in itself, was an obvious sign of *my* need for *her*. Although, as you already know, that wasn't something I could ever admit easily, if at all.

So with each payment I sent, I felt some small satisfaction in knowing one more month had passed without her finding anyone to replace me. Good, good, I'd exult. Let her find out there aren't so many love bargains around. Let her think a little wistfully about me, about what we once had. Let her do a little nibbling at the fancy hors d'oeuvres she may pick up here and there and learn how poorly they compare.

But when it came right down to it, I didn't really care much for the idea of her nibbling either. Naturally I knew she was seeing other men. I received regular reports from our friends. For some incredible reason, they thought I'd want to know about every sonofabitch she went out with. And I *did*, damn it. The hurt was so exquisitely sweet I wouldn't have missed it for anything. Neurotic? Of course. But it's not at all an unusual syndrome. Any man or woman who has ever been in love has suffered from it, and knowing and understanding about it doesn't help. When it came my turn, I was no different.

The thing was, Norman, my not being married to my wife anymore didn't automatically make me stop loving her. All it did was make me stop living and fighting with her. And if anything, this allowed me to love her even more, since the memory of the bad quickly fades, while sentiment and nostalgia make the good seem far better than it may have been. So there I was, floating in that special lovers' purgatory reserved for those condemned to envisioning the ones they love in the arms of others. And I hung there. And each time I heard about Barbara going out with another man, I assaulted myself with these godawful visions of her laughing at the miserable bastard's jokes, of her looking at him with those warm, loving eyes, of her letting him take her to bed and touch and know the body that only I had touched and known for so long. And I was very good at this kind of mental movie. I not only saw it in full, painful detail, I saw it all in color.

I don't mean to imply that I sat home brooding every night. I did my own fair share of running around. Right after the bust-up, I think I was trying to screw anything that moved. It was pure compulsion. I needed to affirm my right to life. And for pure affirmation, sex is about the best we have. Make love, and death is for others, never for you. Make love, and failure is far away. Make love, and pain and despair are gone. Make love, and you'll never be alone and weeping in the night.

So I had a pretty fair go at it for a while. Some were almost embarrassingly young. They could have been my daughters. They had perfect bodies, perfect skin. Maybe too perfect. There's a very subtle point where the perfection of flesh becomes curiously like the perfection of foam rubber. I had forgotten how such flesh could be. I had also forgotten how often the young mistake energy and enthusiasm and pure lust, for sensuality. I guess the last time I was in bed with anyone that young, I was too young myself to be able to see the difference. Back then, I think I was just dazzled, not only by the absolute wonder of the act itself, but by my own gratitude.

But I had all ages to help me celebrate, or rather,

mourn my divorce—not just the young. Although I must admit that at the beginning, the younger ones were the more tempting. Besides, Norman, I was curious. All I knew about them, so far, was from hearsay, and I felt I deserved to find out a few things for myself. It wasn't entirely pleasing. And the older ones, in turn, offered a fair share of different irritants. If they had never been married, if they had been floating around the singles scene for ten or fifteen years, they carried the mark of it. They were too practiced, too smooth, too glossy. Everything they said and did, in bed or out, I was sure had been said and done precisely the same way a hundred times before, with a hundred different men. Maybe I'm being unfair, but this was how they came across to me and how I reacted.

If some of these older women *had* been married before—and, God forgive me, I'm actually talking about those around *forty* as older women—they carried their own assortment of problems. Whether divorced or widowed, they usually turned out to be a little too bitter, or a little too angry, or a little too eager, or a little too desperate. And often I found myself feeling sorry for them, which is probably the saddest thing of all, and the most hopeless, as far as any chance of romance is concerned. I'd look at them and talk to them and touch them and lie with them, and I'd know exactly what they were thinking and feeling every step of the way. They wanted so desperately to love and be loved, to grab for another chance, to prove themselves able to do better at what they may have failed at before, that it tore my heart out just to be near them.

Jesus, I hope I don't sound superior about this, Norman. I never considered myself better as a man than they were as women. In many ways I felt myself to be in a lot worse shape. All I'm trying to get across here are my own very personal reactions to situations, to relationships into which I was thrown and in which I was never really comfortable or happy. And one of my problems here was my lack of coolness. I mean, man, *I was not cool!* How I wished I weren't so damned emotionally hot and sweaty and caring about everyone and everything. How I wished I could be pleasantly above it all, or failing that, then at least so involved that I wasn't aware of what was going on every second. And hurting because of it.

Well-meaning friends often had a way of surprising me with dates I neither knew about nor wanted. I'd be invited to dinner and there'd just happen to be an unattached female beside me at the table. Which was unfair, both to the woman and to me. Because interested or not, my nature was such that I instantly felt myself saddled with this terrible sense of obligation to my unrequested date. I felt I had to at least *appear* interested. I didn't want her to feel less than desirable. I didn't want to hurt her by making her think I didn't find her utterly captivating, with the result that I'd sometimes end up hurting her far more by leading her to believe there was hope for us as a couple, when there really wasn't.

With one woman, a gentle, sweet-faced young widow whose husband had died of a cerebral hemorrhage, I actually went through four dates and a sexual debacle before I was finally able to get it across to her that we had no future together. She was lovely,

Norman, but just not for me, and by that time there were tears, anger, and recriminations. And all because I wasn't *cool* enough. All because I was too concerned about her feelings to let her know at once that although our hosts may have had only the best of intentions, they had done neither of us a favor by trying to play Cupid.

But worst of all, and what probably did more than anything else to spoil these other women for me, was the fact that I was so inescapably Barbara-haunted. Divorced or not, I couldn't seem to get rid of my wife. Talking to a woman, I'd remember some pet phrase of Barbara's, or a way she had of trailing off her words, or of raising her voice with surprise, and from that moment on I'd be glassy-eyed and only half there. Or having dinner with a woman, I'd get hung up watching the way she handled her silver. Why? Because Barbara had somehow managed to bring a greater quality of grace to the essentially unattractive act of eating than anyone I've ever known. Or at the movies with a woman, I'd keep waiting for her to laugh, or look at me, or reach for my hand at precisely the moment Barbara might have done each of these things. Or in bed with a woman, what evolved was a perpetual *ménage à trois*. There were always three of us there, with Barbara either sitting at the foot of the bed, watching with amused eyes, or jumping in to spoil a climactic moment, or distracting me so badly I was embarrassed to find my performance suffering. And although the psychiatrist in me knew exactly what was happening, it didn't do me one damn bit of good as a man. At these moments

my wife was the devil incarnate. So what I really
needed was an exorcist.

Since you've never met my wife, Norman, since
all you know about her is what I've told you in these
tapes, I'm not sure how well I've done at getting
across the kind of effect she had on me, or how much
I really cared about her. It was an odd thing, Norman, but for a man who always created an image of
such great self-sufficiency, of such enormous emotional strength, I couldn't even bear to be without
some contact with my wife. If I was separated from
her for a few days, a week, two weeks, there would
always come a moment when I absolutely *had* to call
her. Not to say or ask anything in particular. Just to
hear her voice. The feeling was so strong, it was
almost physical. There was nothing special about her
voice. It was just a voice. But it had the ability to
flash straight into me like a drug shot. Sometimes it
could actually give me a winner's strength, cram me
full of confidence, hope, wit. At such moments there
was nothing that wasn't possible for me. Even though
I might hardly think of her for days at a time, I could
suddenly fall into a black period where I despised myself, what I was doing, and everything about my life,
and I had to hold her and feel her holding me. If I
couldn't hold her then, I'd be like an addict waiting
for his needle.

My wife was fluent in the language of love. She
was its intimate. What she felt, she was able to say,
which I could never do. So, it was no small thing to
me. She also knew about love and dying. Once, a
long time ago, when we lay together after making

love, when we were filled with the moment and with each other and with that lovers' passionate arrogance that lets you believe that no one else has ever quite had and felt what you've just had and felt, she said, "I think I'm more afraid of dying at this moment than ever before in my life."

Of course she was. At that moment she felt she had the most to lose, as we both did.

But of the two of us, it was always my wife who had the greater sense of mortality, the more conscious awareness that death lurked in love's shadow. When we argued, when she was most furious with me, it was usually about this. "You're the smartest man in the world," she once railed, "yet you don't know *anything*. Do you think you're going to live forever?"

"No," I admitted.

"Then when are you going to start *living*?" she asked.

"I'm living," I said.

"Like hell you are!" she shouted. "All you're doing is working, damn you. And by your twisted way of reasoning, you think that's living. You think that's enough. You think that's everything."

At that point, I decided it was better to remain quiet.

"Don't you know you're going to die?" she asked, and she was crying now. "Don't you know you're going to wake up dying one morning and wonder where it all went?"

And I still said nothing.

"Don't you know how much I love you?" she said.

And miserably, because I knew where she was heading, and because I knew she was right all the way, I nodded.

"Don't you *care* that I love you?" she pressed on.

And I nodded my head again. My God, how I cared. Yet all I could do was move my head up and down, up and down like a monkey on a string.

"Then please act that way," she pleaded. "Please show me before it's too late. Please start living with me. *Please!* Because I don't want to put it off anymore. I don't want to wake up dying one morning along with you, and have to wonder where it all went. Except I won't really have to wonder, will I? I'll know. It'll all be broken up, split into a thousand tiny pieces, and buried in your goddamn patients."

She hated my patients with as much passion as she loved me. It was a wild, irrational kind of jealousy, but I understood it. She felt I was never free of them, never took time off, never went on vacations, never did things with her that other husbands allegedly did with their wives. She claimed that even when I was with her, I was only partly with her. "Less than half," was how she once described it. "At any given time, even when you're with me, the best part of you is somewhere else. You throw me the dregs, the worst parts. And it's always less than half."

I understood what she felt, but that didn't mean I was always so understanding. If I was feeling confident and controlled, if I was reasonably pleased with myself and the way my work was going, I could take my whipping without much fuss. But God help her *and* me if she got me when things weren't going so well, if I was under heavy pressure from some patients, if I felt rushed and panicked about time. Then I wouldn't just sit there while she harangued me with her list of grievances. Then I'd hit back, hard and dirty. I'd tell her to get the hell off my goddamn back. I'd tell her my work was the single most important thing in my life, and if she didn't like it, that was too bad because I wasn't about to change any part of it. I'd call her a narcissistic, self-indulgent, pleasure-seeking bitch who thought only about herself.

Then if she still kept at me, and if I was going through a particularly hard time in the office or at the hospital, I'd *really* get mean. Sometimes I'd even get low, deepdown, anti-Semitic mean, which is the ultimate meanness, the ultimate stupidity for one Jew to pour over another Jew. I'd accuse her of being an archetypical, ball-breaking Jewish female who couldn't be happy unless she was emasculating her husband and eating him alive. Once I actually went so far as to compare her to the female praying mantis, which I apparently must have decided was also Jewish, and which has the selfishly discomforting habit of biting off the head of her mate as he copulates with her and then of eating the rest of him once she's inseminated. My wife and the praying mantis, a couple of nice Jewish girls.

And these are just a few of the things I'd say, Norman, to the woman I loved more than anyone on this earth. And why did I say them? Well, the silly, presumptuous woman actually had the nerve to want me to spend a little more time just being with her and loving her.

October 24

I'M GOING TO HAVE TO ASK your indulgence, Norman. I had several things I planned to talk to you
about today, a few abstract concepts of love that I
thought might be significant, or at least of interest.
But the only thing I really feel like talking about
right now is my wife. And whatever concepts of love
may be involved aren't going to be at all abstract.

I've tried not to think too much about it, but I still
keep wondering about Barbara's reaction when she
learns what's happening to me. I also keep wondering
whether I'm really doing the right thing in not letting
her know, in shutting her out of it. I mean the right
thing for *her*. I know myself and my motives—at

least I think I do. In my own way, I guess I'm just trying to punish her, although I don't really know for what. Unless it's for the sin of loving me too much. Or else for simply having understood more about it than I did.

One of the most important things my wife understood about love, Norman, was that you do it *now*, not yesterday or tomorrow. A fact that very few of us, including myself, ever truly realize. And because we don't realize it, we fantasize the whole thing and drown it in sentiment. And the sentiment is false. It's false because it's not our own. We read love stories in books. We see love stories on the screen and on the stage. And we exult in the joys of the make-believe lovers and weep for their sorrows. Yet when it comes to our own, when we're dealing with our *own* wives or husbands, our *own* lovers, our *own* parents, our *own* children, all those closest to and most dependent on us for their love, we suddenly seem to be turned to stone.

The sad fact of it is, we've gotten to be spectators in regard to so many other things, that we're getting to be spectators with love as well, observers rather than participants. As long as we fantasize love, we're able to feel it consciously and deeply. But when it comes to our own personal involvements, when it comes to our own *real* love, we frequently don't even know what's going on. Or, if we do know, we can't respond to it. Or, if we *can* respond to it, we respond out of some nostalgic memory of what took place somewhere back in the past, rather than because of what's happening right now.

Barbara would know exactly what was going on every minute. And sometimes she'd let *me* know too, which ended up making me defensive and causing another of our battles. I remember one night when we were driving home from seeing a movie. I forget the name of the picture, but it was a nostalgic film about the fifties that exploited precisely the kind of absorption with the past that I'm talking about. And I had really enjoyed it. It had left me in a warm, mellow mood, and I responded by recalling the early days of our own love and marriage and some of the wonderful things, some of the wonderful experiences and feelings we had shared. To which my wife replied, "Baloney!"

I was surprised. "*Weren't* they wonderful times?" I asked.

"Yes," she said. "But *you* never knew it. You were never even remotely aware of it. Not then, anyway."

"Why not?" I said, too pleasantly lulled by the movie, or too abstracted, or too stupid to notice what I was walking into.

"Because you're you," she told me quietly. "Because even back then you were you."

"And what's that supposed to mean?" I asked.

"It means that even back then," she said, "you lived in your own little vacuum. You didn't know what kind of joy we had, what kind of love, what kind of marvelous moments. Your mind and thoughts were always with other things. If it wasn't the problems at the hospital during your residency, it was the problems with getting through your boards. And when the boards were behind you, it was building up your practice that worried and held you twenty-four hours a day. And when your practice was finally twice that of the average shrink, it was struggling to keep up with it that drove you to the wall."

My fine, mellow mood was gone. "Forgive me," I told her. "I guess I should have been a pimp or a playboy and just concentrated on being aware of the joys of loving you."

"I never asked for that," she said. "But it does seem a shame you're never going to know what you have until it's gone and you don't have it anymore."

My wife was right, of course, Norman. But that never stopped me from getting up on my hind legs and roaring and chewing her head off each time she pointed out my deficiencies. In fact, if she *hadn't* been so damn right, I might have been less angry and argued less.

So in the midst of our love, we fought. And in the midst of our fighting, we made love. The more we fought, the more bitter and violent our battles, the more intense became our love making. It wasn't really illogical. It's in the textbooks. Love brings both joy and destruction, and sex is the classic means of holding off the fear and threat of death. In our case, it was the threatened death of our marriage we were trying to hold off. And the closer we came to it, the more obsessively we went at each other in bed.

It was a startling thing, Norman. I know there's no such thing as sexual perfection. Each experience, when it's right, can be new and exciting in its own way. But I think what we started to have at the end, even after so many years together, was about as close to the best as it's possible to get. We never talked about it at all while it was still going on. It was almost as though we were afraid to mention it, afraid that talking about it would somehow cause it to end. Finally we did talk about it once, and it was finished right there. Of course we didn't know it at the time, nor did either of us consciously intend it that way. But that was the last time we were ever to make love together.

I guess it was Barbara who started it. I was just lying there, trying not to think about anything, when she got out of bed for a cigarette then came back to lie beside me.

"It's been good, hasn't it?" she said. Barbara wasn't generally what you'd call a soft-spoken woman, Norman, but her voice was barely audible then.

I nodded. I think I must have still been a little wary of giving my own voice to it.

"Why?" she asked.

"I don't know," I lied.

"Am I much better at it than I was at the beginning?" she wanted to know.

"Much better," I told her and didn't have to lie this time.

"So are you," she told me. "I can't imagine a man being any better. Although I'm no authority on such things."

"You're an authority," I assured her. "You can take my word for it."

She laughed. "We never really had any trouble in bed, did we?" she said.

"No," I said.

She didn't say the rest of it. She didn't have to.

"I love you," she told me.

"I know," I said. "And I love you."

"Isn't that sad," she said. And though it was dark and I couldn't see her face, I had the feeling she was crying.

And that was pretty much the end of it. A few days later we had our worst fight of all, and by mutual agreement I moved out for good.

Of course I've said it before in these tapes, Norman; it's all temporary anyway. With or without love, we finally leave one another. It's just that the leaving hurts a lot more when we love. Still, I don't think I'd have wanted that part any different. I may have done some hurting, but at least I *felt*. For which I'm grateful. Lack of feeling is still the ultimate tragedy. So I guess I've been pretty lucky in that respect.

Not that I've always felt especially lucky. Certainly not lately, and certainly not about my wife. Sometimes, lying in the darkness, I think about her, although I don't always start it consciously. Last night it started with a dream. Barbara was there, leaning over me. But when I reached up for her, she was gone. And I was awake and alone. Yet she seemed to have left all sorts of things behind, a few of her expressions, the way her hair drifted over one cheek, a soft laugh, an off-key whistle. I seemed to see her more clearly last night, Norman, than I ever did when she was with me. Everything seemed blown up, larger than life. I could actually imagine the particular way her lips felt, the softness at the base of her throat, the curve of her waist under my hand, an old dress she wore for years simply because she knew I loved what it did to her breasts.

Moments came back when we were together in bed—some, at the very beginning, when she was young and just finding out what was possible, her flesh firm, her mind bright and willing to learn, her mouth eager to carry out orders, her arms reaching and never quite having enough. Her eyes came back to search things out, to punish me. I had drifted off into another life. I had refused to take her along. Why? She had asked nothing more than to share with me. Where was the threat? I tried to picture only the good things—there were so many. I lay in the darkness for a long time, thinking of them.

So there I was, doing exactly what I usually did, what she so often accused me of doing—burying my head in the past, wrapping myself in nostalgia, while the present drifted quietly away from me. And now, even in this particular present, my last, I still refuse to take her along. I'm dying without her. I listen to the words of cheap, sentimental love songs on the radio while I fast run out of past *and* present.

October 25

I WISH I WERE BETTER PREPARED for dying, Norman.
I wish I had something more to prop me up along the
way, perhaps a few reassuring religious convictions,
or comforting philosophical concepts, or maybe even
the belief that there might be something more await-
ing me than just nothing. I know that may sound a
bit strange, coming from a psychiatrist. It's supposed
to be part of our business to know about such things.
We are, after all, regularly called upon to ease the
mental and emotional anguish brought on by death
and dying. And I've always felt I've done a pretty
fair job along that line. It's just that I can't seem to
use any of our regular stock of bromides for myself.

They're too glib and simplistic, too banal. They're too lacking in conviction. But I'm afraid it's mostly that I just don't have the necessary faith.

I remember a few years ago a Catholic neighbor of mine died. The guy was appallingly young and left behind a wife and five small kids. They were a great family and I cared about them. I was deeply affected, which must have showed, because when I stopped in one evening to offer my condolences to the widow, it was *she* who comforted *me*. "Please don't be so sad," she said. "I'm sure Johnny is happy tonight. Even if he had the chance to come back to us, I'm sure he'd much rather stay where he is." And she wasn't just saying it; she believed every word.

Well, I thought that was pretty great for the bereaved widow. And I still do. The Catholic religion does offer about as good a package in that area as you're likely to find. The catch is, you've got to be able to believe it. You have to be able to accept as fact what you can neither see nor understand. Which means you have to be able to suspend all thought, all knowledge, all contrary evidence and mold your own small icon of belief out of just the emotions. And I never could.

I'm not trying to be lofty about this. I don't consider myself *above* religious belief, just *incapable* of it. That doesn't mean I haven't indulged in some vaguely religious hocus-pocus of my own. As a matter of fact, Norman, I've done precisely that every night of my life since I was six years old and my father first taught me the *shma yisrael*, a brief Hebrew prayer that I have never once missed reciting to myself before going to sleep. It's true. Regardless of where I've been or with whom, I've never closed my eyes for the night without first going through this small, mental ritual, which I address specifically to God and in which I request care, guidance, and reasonably decent treatment for myself and all those I love, both living and dead. And since I allegedly don't acknowledge the existence of any God nor practice any religion, this surely has to be considered one of the craziest bits yet.

I have my explanations for it, of course. My favorite one is that it provides me with a continuing tie to my father, since he was the one who got me started on the ritual. This reduces it to just another small fragment of filial nostalgia. Then comes my number two explanation, which has more to do with the whole concept of Jewish tradition and my otherwise total neglect of it. What the hell, I tell myself, I'm still a Jew, aren't I? I can't just lightly toss away five thousand years of history and blood.

And finally, there's my big, back-up explanation, and this has to do with God Himself. Since I tend to be an outspokenly irreverent type, having once, in great anger, gone so far as to claim that if there *were* indeed a God, He would have to be a Committee, because no single God could possibly have messed things up this badly, and since I have all that stuff weighted so heavily against me, I figured it can't possibly hurt if I lean over and hold out my hand in the darkness for a few seconds each night. I mean, like hey, man! You never can tell what you might accidentally *touch*.

Like most of us, I guess, I've spent my whole life looking for something outside my own limitations, outside my own small humanness, to believe in. And love of God is the one thing that seems to come with our territory. It's as basic to us as the need for our parents when we're small. Pitifully helpless in the face of time, life, death, and eternity, we desperately seek some Great Father to give meaning and order to the often confused, painful, and empty days of our lives. We don't *want* to believe—we *hate* to believe—we can't *allow* ourselves to believe there's no true reason or pattern to it, that it's all just struggle, struggle, goodby, and nothingness. We want and need some Big Daddy up there somewhere to love us, to kiss and reward us when we're good, to punish us when we're bad, and to let us finally believe that everything that happens in our brief passing through does so for some worthwhile purpose. And since no one has ever really given Him to us, we've had to invent Him. Yet such a thing can't really be a group project. It's much too personal. So, we've all had to invent him separately, each for ourselves.

Except that we don't seem to have done too good a job of it, judging from the results so far. I remember hearing as a child that God had created each of us in His own image, and later thinking, as I grew older and more aware of the nature of things, that if this were indeed so, then He must be pretty damn cruel and vicious. So apparently my blasphemy started at a very early age. But if it did, it was only because I cared so intensely, was so desperate in my search for some evidence of His reason and goodness and love, that each new discovery to the contrary, each new disappointment, only caused me to overreact in my anger.

Jesus, was I furious with God! The things that were done in His name, the abominations committed with *His* religion, with the worship of *Him* as its justification. The bloodbaths of the Crusades, the horrors of the Inquisition, the Christians murdering the Moslems, the Moslems murdering the Christians, the Catholics and Protestants murdering each other, and the same with the Hindus and Moslems. And, of course, everyone getting together and murdering the Jews. And all in *His* name, all in the conviction that this was in *His* best interests, all in the unswerving belief that this was what *He* wanted.

When I was a kid, I wrote out lists of such abominations. One was, EVIDENCE THAT GOD IS CRUEL. Another said, SIGNS THAT GOD DOESN'T LOVE ANYONE AT ALL. And still another list was headed, PROOF THAT THERE IS NO GOD. My lists were long, terrible, and, to me at least, frighteningly conclusive. And, oh, how badly they made me feel. How I fought against accepting history's evidence. How desperately I wanted to believe in the existence of God and to love Him and have Him love me. To this end, I even composed other lists which I hoped would give me supporting arguments. These lists were entitled: EVIDENCE THAT GOD IS LOVING AND GOOD, and SIGNS THAT THERE REALLY IS A GOD. I did manage to scrape together a few such points on the positive side, but I had to dig hard and it was never really any contest.

Still, I continued to hang in there, Norman, trying

to give Him the benefit of every doubt, urging Him on in the mental whisper of my little *shma yisrael* prayer each night, searching him out in some particular sunset, probing for signs in peak experiences, in dreams, in mystic sounds, in music, in the miracle of birth, in the healing of wounds. I pleaded for hope in selfless acts, in anonymous charity, in tests of courage, in the wonder of sacrifice, in the capacity for bearing pain, reaching for documentation in the incredible shape of an ear, in the wonder of an eye, in the complexities of the brain—and actually coming closest, almost truly believing in and touching Him during very special moments of love.

Then the full, irrefutable evidence of the Holocaust began coming to light and forced me to drink, swallow, and breathe in its poison.

I'm not sure of exactly how old I was when this ultimate obscenity clobbered me. I guess I must have been somewhere in my early teens. Whatever my age, I was old enough to read the accounts and stories, and to see the actual films of the death camps. And I felt the sickness start deep in my gut and spread until it was all I could feel. And I remember weeping one night and pleading aloud—I don't know to whom, Norman—but just begging someone, *anyone*, "Please, please let there *not* be a God." Because I was sure I wouldn't have been able to bear it if I thought there *had* been a God, and He had permitted, had sanctioned, had indeed given His blessing to such horror.

Of course that was many years ago. I'm older now. And much of what happened under the Germans has been forgotten or forgiven. But it still burns in my gut. It will until I die. And if I was ever tempted, in some confused and weakening moment of human compassion, to soften my stand, I had only to remember a documentary account I once read of what happened to 1½ million Jewish children under the age of sixteen in those German camps. In one way or another, they all died. But a few particular sentences from that story have stayed with me over the years. I think I must have memorized them. They said, "After that the guard told the children to take off their clothes, fold them neatly, and march into the gas chamber. One little boy—he must have been under two years old—was too small to climb the steps. So the guard picked the child up in his arms and carried him into the chamber."

That child, that one little boy, became and remained my conclusive evidence of the absence of God.

Yet I went on, yet I go on still, even now, saying my little prayer each night, sending it off into the silent dark like a tiny Hebrew radar beam in search of divinity. So apparently I never stopped looking, not even with my patients. Sometimes I'd listen to them talk—the openly religious ones, the closet clerics, the agnostics, the atheists—all taking their separate paths, but all seeking the same vision of God. And they expected definitive answers from their shrink, from *me*. While I, in turn, though they didn't know, sought answers from them. Some said there *must* be a God, others that there *may* be, still others denied even the possibility. But they all agreed on one thing: Whatever God there might be, whatever form

He took if He did exist, whatever precepts he embodied, foremost among them would have to be that of love. In all their visions, this remained the single, immutable constant.

If I tried to create a single voice describing a composite vision of God, an image put together from the hopes, dreams, and imagination of hundreds of patients in countless therapy sessions over the years, it would probably come out sounding something like this: "God loves me. He sees and knows everything. There's no way I can hide from Him. But I wouldn't want to hide from Him even if I could, because He looks after me. Even when I do something wrong, He still loves me. Nothing can make Him stop loving me. He accepts me for what I am. He doesn't sit in judgment upon me. He loves me no matter what. When I think of dying, I'm afraid, but I'm less afraid when I remember that God loves me and I'm going to join Him when I die. I'd feel lost without God's love. When everything else goes wrong, when nothing seems to mean anything, I remember that God loves me and I feel better. When I love, when I love anyone or anything, that's when I feel closest to God. Without God, there could be no love. When I love, I feel a small part of God inside me. When I love, He loves me, I love Him and I feel we're one."

So finally, Norman, even in that, it seems to come out all love. Even when we claim not to believe, even when we claim we're just imagining, what we evidently imagine most about Him is His love. How confused we are about the whole thing. Perhaps me, most of all. I reason too much. I've studied too much about the principles of logic, which is probably the greatest handicap, the greatest weight of all to carry when you know you're dying. Logic is a ton load around your neck. It never lets up. It never allows you rest or true peace.

Do you know what I'd like most right now, Norman? That is, other than to hear a news bulletin announcing a sudden, new cure for leukemia? I'd like to be able to suspend all reason, shut out entirely the effects of a lifetime of logic. I'd like to be able to believe that just before I finally push off, during those last few moments when I'm half here and half there, that I'll open my eyes for one final look around and see it all, that I'll be able to understand everything *wasn't* really just a series of insane accidents, that I didn't just do what I did and love those I loved purely by chance, that I'll finally know there *was* a specific plan to it all, a subtle design woven into it with the sure hand of a Master Craftsman—and that even the bad, the terrible, the worst of things were there for some reason, for some better purpose than was ever visible before.

Wouldn't that be nice?

So you see how it finally is, Norman, how it finally becomes for us? In dying, we allow ourselves the luxury of a kind of make-believe we'd never have allowed ourselves in living. It's the ultimate opiate, the greatest pain-killer of them all. There isn't a drug on the market that can match it. So if I sometimes think I have to take this all pretty much cold turkey, it isn't entirely true. I do have my own special ways to make it easier. I do have my little nightly prayer that I refuse to call a prayer, addressed to a God I refuse to admit exists. I do have my composite image of the divine presence of love, all-embracing and nonjudgmental. And finally, I do have my own marvelous little fantasy of those last mortal moments, in which everything becomes as clear, as glowing, as orderly, and as upbeat as the concluding episode of an old *Saturday Evening Post* serial.

So I guess it's at least manageable.

October 27

———

SOMETHING HAS HAPPENED since I last spoke to you, Norman. I don't think it will surprise you. Checking back over my last few tapes, I seem to have been tossing hints all over the place about what was coming. But I must have done it subconsciously, because I don't think I was really aware of it. Anyway, what I did was call my wife the other day.

Of course, I had to pretend to her as well as to myself that I was calling about something else, something involving the children. You see, I've used a rather complicated story these past weeks to keep Barbara and the kids from knowing about me. I won't bother you with details, but it involved my allegedly being off somewhere on an extended lecture tour. And since I had my practice and everything else pretty well covered, there was no reason for suspicion on her part. Nor did I say anything on the phone that was likely to make her wonder about the call. Yet I was talking to her for no more than a few minutes, and rolling along just fine with my pretenses, when she suddenly asked me what was wrong.

"Nothing is wrong," I told her. "Why should anything be wrong?"

"I don't know," she said. I didn't say anything. "But you do sound kind of strange," she told me.

"Maybe that's because I'm an estranged husband," I said.

"Oh, Jesus!" she said. "Your jokes are as bad as ever."

"I guess I haven't been practicing much lately," I said.

She asked me again, "What's wrong?"

"Well . . ." I said. Then I stopped and just stared at the phone while the whole thing clotted in my throat. "I seem to have gotten myself a little bit sick."

"How little?" she asked.

I took a deep breath and slowly let it out. At that moment, Norman, I swear I was six years old again and about to confess to my mother that I felt feverish and couldn't go out to play. "I'm afraid it's not really so little," I told her.

She said, "What do you mean, not so little?"

"I guess maybe I mean a lot."

"Oh, damn it!" she said and sounded angry. Which was how she always sounded when she was frightened.

"I'm sorry," I said.

"Oh, you miserable bastard!" she said. "I knew it, I knew it. The minute I heard your goddamn voice I knew it."

I laughed. I felt better already.

"What's so funny?" she shouted.

"You," I told her. "I had almost forgotten how you could be."

"I'm coming right over," she said.

"You don't have to do that," I told her.

"Like hell I don't," she yelled.

Then for a minute, Norman, I panicked. I didn't know if I really wanted to see her. I wasn't sure I could handle it. Then it passed and I said all right.

When I hung up the phone, my hand was shaking. I was in a sweat. I felt like a kid who had just arranged for his first date. And I prepared myself the same way. I shaved, I fretted that my hair needed cutting. I fussed with it. I studied myself in the mirror and wondered how bad I really looked. Then I settled back to wait for her. I was so anxious, it made me angry with myself. What the hell was the matter with me, I wondered. I kept asking myself the same dumb question over and over again. Which was pretty silly, because I knew very well what was the matter with me. I simply didn't want to make an ass of myself. I didn't want to do or say anything stupid. I didn't want to strip myself naked in front of her. I didn't want to dissipate my reserves. And I wasn't at all sure I'd be able to keep myself from doing any or all of these things.

Yet the moment she came in, the moment I saw

the way she looked, all I was worried about was her. Her face was pale. She was obviously frightened. She didn't know what to expect. We looked at each other and neither of us knew quite what to say. My face ached, Norman, literally, just from trying to keep it looking as pleasant and healthy as possible. Carefully dressed, combed, and shaved, I guess I didn't really look so bad because she said, "Hey, who are you trying to kid? You never looked better in your life."

All I seemed able to do was stare at her and grin. Emotion choked me. My God, I thought. What have I learned? I'm at the end of my life and I've learned nothing. Not a damn thing. I look at this woman and I may as well be twenty years old again. Nothing I've done has even started to prepare me for this.

"Listen," she said. "As long as I've known you, you've never been sick. I've never even seen you in a robe and slippers. You don't even own them. You don't even own a pair of *pajamas*, for God's sake!"

"Absolutely," I agreed. "I've always been a very healthy type. A well-running machine. You know me. I wouldn't allow any tarnish on my perfect image. And sick was imperfect."

"And now?" she asked.

"And now," I said, "I find I'm very imperfect."

Then she looked at me for a long time, Norman, and became frightened again, and I knew what was coming. "All right," she said. "What's wrong with you?"

"Please understand," I told her. "That isn't why I called you. I didn't call you to tell you how sick I am."

She said it again. "What's wrong with you?"

I felt as if I were about to go off a very high place. Then I told her.

Characteristically, she responded with anger. "What the hell are you talking about?"

"I'm sorry," I said.

"What do you mean, you're sorry?" she yelled at me. "Stop being so goddamned sorry all the time."

The use of profanity was comparatively new for her. She had never been very good at it but was clearly improving.

"Okay," I told her. "I'll stop being so goddamned sorry."

"You sonofabitch!" she yelled. "You're only forty-two goddamn years old!"

She started to cry then. Her face got all twisted up and I didn't know where to look.

"Damn you!" she swore through her tears. "It wasn't enough to tear my insides out for so many years? Now you've got to do *this* to me too?"

I grinned. I was able to enjoy it a little by then. I said, "Don't take it so personally. Actually, I had no intention of telling you about it at all."

She stared at me with those terrific green eyes, which are terrific even when they're crying, and there aren't many eyes that can manage that. "Are you serious?" she asked. "You really *weren't* going to tell me?"

I nodded.

"You hated me *that* much?" she said.

"I've never hated you," I told her. "I've felt a lot of things for you, but hate was never one of them."

"Then why would you try to shut me out of this?" she asked. "How could you even *want* to?"

"It wasn't a question of shutting you out," I said. "I just didn't want you to have to go through it with me. I saw no point to it. It wasn't as if we were still living together. Since you were no longer that closely involved with my life, why should I have to get you involved with my death?"

She looked at me as though I had hit her. She pressed her hands to her face and the tears flowed through her fingers. I sat watching her cry as I had so many times before—when our parents were dying, when she learned she couldn't conceive, when we fought most bitterly, when we decided to separate, when our divorce became final. Now I was dying and I was sitting and watching her cry again. She looked small, almost frail, as she wept, and it surprised me, Norman. I had never thought of Barbara as a frail woman. But I guess she is.

"Why don't you tell me the truth?" she said.

"What's the truth?" I asked.

"That you wanted to punish me," she said.

"For what?" I asked.

"For failing you as a wife," she said.

I sat silently on that one for awhile. Then I said, "If that was some small part of my reason at the beginning, it wasn't for very long. There's one thing about being terminal. It makes you think. And most of what I've been thinking about has been us and our life together. If anyone did the failing there, it was much less you than I. If I didn't know that before, I know it now. So what can I tell you? That if I had another chance at it, I'd do it differently? All right. I'd do it differently. But we both know I probably wouldn't, that I'd probably do the same stupid things all over again. I'm a terrible learner. The only thing I seem to have learned these past weeks is that I never learned anything."

She wiped her eyes and face with the back of her hand. "Oh, stop being so damned humble and contrite," she said. "I'm not used to you that way. I don't think I even *like* you that way. Besides, you're awful at it."

"Well," I said, "I told you I was a terrible learner."

She sighed and her eyes were still wet, but she had stopped crying. "How much time do we have?" she asked.

"I don't know," I told her.

"How much time?" she repeated.

I gave her an approximation.

"All right," she said.

"All right, what?" I asked.

"All right," she said. "Are you going to just sit there like a *shmuck*, or are you going to kiss me?"

I kissed her, Norman.

October 29

Yesterday was a rough one for me, Norman, one of the worst yet. I told my children.

I knew it would finally have to come, of course. There was no reasonable way to avoid it. But that didn't make it one bit easier when the moment arrived. Whatever I may know of such things, I know of no way to truly prepare yourself. The heartland is still pretty much an uncharted wilderness. So far, we're just skimming its edges. It's easy to get lost there.

I decided it would be best to tell my son and daughter separately, one at a time. It's not something you can share. You take it alone. And I certainly didn't want each of them having to worry about the possible reactions of the other. I had my wife arrange to leave me alone with Judi first.

I've told you a little about my son, Norman, but I don't think I've mentioned much, if anything, about my daughter. It's an odd thing. When I first conceived the idea for these tapes—in fact even after I had started the actual taping—I didn't expect to be personalizing them as much as I have. I expected to be dealing more with the general psychological concepts of love than with my own personal involvements with it. Obviously, I changed my mind, or rather, my own needs got into the act and changed it *for* me. In any case, the thing grew so haphazardly, so without plan, that I just rambled on as I happened to feel when I had the microphone in my hand.

So, if I haven't brought my daughter into this until now, I want you to know it wasn't intentional. It wasn't because she was ever any less a part of my life and love than her brother and mother. In fact, if I had to come up with a particular reason for neglecting her in these tapes, I'd probably say it was because I felt less guilty about Judi than I did about David and my wife, and therefore less needful of confession and self-flagellation. Because, my God, have I been beating myself! For which, incidentally, I'm not apologizing. I obviously needed it. And since these tapes are *my* indulgence, since I'm doing them to satisfy my own needs, that's about all the justification required. But I'm happy to say I think I did pretty well with Judi. No sack cloth and ashes for me as a father to *her*.

Unlike my son, Judi was always a communicator. What she felt, she was always able to say. From the time she was old enough to say the word *love*, she delighted in just saying how much she loved me. And like the typically vain father of a sweet, adoring female child, I responded by saying how much *I* loved *her*. When she wanted or needed something, she was able to ask me for it. And because she asked, I gave. She has revealed herself to be a lonely and dependent girl, but she knows how to be obliging and appealing and this has made it easier for her. It has also made it easier for me to be a gracious, loving, and attentive father to her. Another thing she knows is the importance of being able to say she's sorry. Which is almost as important to your personal salvation, to your defense against loneliness, as being able to say you love.

In a moment of childish frustration and anger, she once told me she wished I were dead, something most children wish for their parents at one time or another. But the difference with Judi was that within minutes after the words were out, she was apologizing, begging for forgiveness and telling me she loved and needed me more than anyone in this whole wide world. How much pain she saved herself. My son has also wished me dead a few times over the years, but has never recanted, has never been able to say he was sorry. I have seen him choking with it. I have seen the anguish in his eyes for days afterward. But I never heard a word of apology from him. About *anything*.

Neither of my children were ever great students, Norman, both of them needed help with their studies, but Judi was the only one who got it from me. Why?

Because she asked for it. It was as simple as that. All she had to do was say, "Daddy, I'm doing awfully with my algebra, please help me." And whatever my schedule, whatever the pressures of my work, I'd somehow find time to help her. My son never said he was doing awfully in anything, never asked for help—in fact refused it when it *was* offered—and failed course after course quietly and without complaint. I'm sure Judi feels as bewildered as David does about being an adopted child, as frightened, as trapped in her own sense of confused and pathless isolation. Yet she talks about it as though it were the best of all possible choices. "I love you so much, Daddy," she has said. "I feel so deliciously *chosen*. I mean, you *picked* me, didn't you? Isn't that better than my just being a crazy kind of birth accident?"

And of course I have assured her that it is indeed better, though I have never believed any part of it— neither the concept of adoption as a joyous thing nor her own particular joy in it. Yet how could I not be touched and moved and filled with love for this loving child who tried so desperately to please me? How could I help but adore this once abandoned, dark-eyed dream, this product of nameless parents who hung onto me as though her life depended on it. Which, in at least an emotional sense, it did. How could I not give whatever I had to give to someone who acted as though she had single-handedly invented the whole notion of love and then had specifically invented me to receive it?

No. As far as Judi is concerned, I carry no guilt. Whatever the reasons, I think I did pretty well for her as a father. Except, perhaps, for the divorce, which I'm sure did neither her nor David very much good. Still, even the divorce didn't affect the way my daughter felt about me. To her, I was still the greatest. She still played up to me outrageously, still called me the handsomest, and smartest, the most loving, the most understanding daddy of them all.

In fact Judi was so well indoctrinated in her understanding of the divorce, so instinctually aware of my own guilt about it, that she actually tried to console me. She would tell me about how many of her friends' parents were divorced, and how it was often better for two people to live apart even though they might still love one another, and that it wasn't a question of it being anyone's fault—it was just the way things happened to work out sometimes. She would soothe me with all the banalities, all the sad little bromides she had heard from either my wife or myself, or that she had read in psychological pamphlets, or that she might have seen on television or in the movies. All she wanted to do was comfort me with love. It was enough to break my heart.

Nevertheless, she once told me, "I wish people could be nicer to one another. I wish people didn't have to fight with one another so much." The "people," of course, were my wife and myself. But that was well after the fact, and it was too late to do anything for her about that particular problem. Besides, I had a far more specific problem to deal with now. I had to tell her she wasn't far from losing me altogether.

I have lost some weight and I tire quickly, but I

have kept my color up with a sunlamp and I can still look pretty good for short periods. So my daughter wasn't really facing any grim spectre when she came to see me. Still, Barbara had done some groundwork by telling her I had been sick and that I had something important to talk to her about, and for someone as sensitive to such things as Judi, this was enough to set off all sorts of little warning signals in her brain.

She seemed tense and nervous from the moment I saw her. I kissed her, I teased her, I talked brightly. I discussed her schoolwork, her tennis program. Incidentally, Norman, the kid is going to be a great player. Tournament caliber. She has the strokes, disposition, motivation—the whole bit. Anyway, she didn't buy much of my sparkling small talk. She just sat there, not quite looking at me, her hands folded in her lap. Then she suddenly started to cry.

"Hey," I said. "What's that for?"

She didn't answer me. She kept her head down and wouldn't even look at me. She's almost fifteen, but small and undeveloped. And when she sat there, all huddled up and crying like that, she looked like a little kid, a lost, frightened waif. That was all I needed. I couldn't even trust myself to speak anymore. I was afraid my voice would crack. My God, I thought, I've got to hold on. I can't make it worse for her than it is.

So I just went to her and I held her. I felt the small fragile bones beneath the fabric of her clothes and fought for control. I thought at first my wife may have tried to spare me by telling Judi herself, but then I knew better. My daughter didn't have to be told by anyone. I have devoted twenty years of my life, Norman, to the allegedly scientific study of the mind and heart, but I'm about ready to put on the robes of a mystic whenever love comes into it. My mother used to talk about something called a "mother's heart." She said a "mother's heart" always knew whether her child was happy or unhappy, well or sick. She claimed that regardless of what anyone said or did, it was impossible to fool a "mother's heart." And for me, at least, it was true. I was never able to fool her. Maybe a daughter's heart works the same way.

"Daddy, don't. . . ." my daughter wept. She didn't say what I shouldn't do. She didn't say I shouldn't die, or that I shouldn't leave her. She just said, "Daddy, don't. . . ." as she might have once said, "Daddy, don't go out tonight," or "Daddy, don't make me go to school today," or "Daddy, don't fight with Mommy anymore." It was that kind of hopeless, pleading effort.

"It's all right," I said and continued to hold her, trying with just my arms and voice to make her feel, amid the immediate disasters I was bringing, that all the good things would still be going on for her, that there would still be love and caring, and others to hold her, and as yet unimagined joys to come.

But it's hard to know these things at age fourteen and a half. It's especially hard to discover the spirit of love in the midst of loss. Sometimes it's not found at all, not at any age. But I hoped then, as I held her, Norman, that my daughter would be one of the lucky ones, that she would somehow manage to find it.

It was a different thing with my son.

You know something about David by now, Norman, so you should be able to understand it. He isn't like Judi. He's usually so deeply inside himself that he doesn't have anything near her perceptions. So he sensed nothing until I told him, until I actually said, in so many words, that in not too long a period of time, I was going to die. And because he sensed nothing, the shock was that much greater. He's also a year younger than Judi and less able to communicate what he feels. Sometimes I'm aware of so much emotion building up inside him, so much he can't let go, that I'm afraid he's going to bust with it. He never confides in me. He rarely confides in anyone. On the rare occasions when he does reveal what he feels and thinks, it's to his mother. Then she tells me.

I know David loves me as much as Judi does, and that he also thinks I'm the living end. But unlike Judi, he has never been able to tell me these things. And because he's the way he is, because he feels so deeply and yet must keep it all bottled up, any pain becomes that much more intense for him. When my son hurts, Norman, he really hurts. Pound for pound, I know of no one with a greater capacity for anguish than my son. And the hell of it is, it's all silent, all invisible.

So when I clubbed him with this, and when it finally broke through to him that in the not too distant future I, his father, would be leaving him for good, all he could do was sit there and stare at me. I didn't even see a change of expression. Which happens to be one of the things about David that has bothered me most over the years. Not only can't he say he's sorry when he knows he has done something wrong, but at the very moment I'm lashing him hardest, that sweet, pink-cheeked face of his remains as free of remorse as it would if he were watching his favorite television show. And this only helped make me angry. I wanted to *see* remorse, damn it! I wanted to *hear* how sorry he was. Never mind what was going on inside him. I reserved my knowledge and proper handling of such things for my patients. With my son, I was no practicing psychiatrist. I was a frustrated and uncertain adoptive father, doubtful of my son's love, guilt-ridden because of my own parental failings and desperately in need of reassurance because of them.

The only time I ever hit my son was at just such a moment of frustration. He absolutely *refused* to say he was sorry for stealing a goddamn bottle of soda from the local delicatessen. He even seemed vaguely amused by my anger, although I knew well enough that he wasn't. But at that moment it was too much for me and I slapped him. And I looked at the marks of my fingers on that beloved but still unrepentent face and thought, my God, what do I want from him? *Blood*?

His face was the same now, although a year or two older. I had just told him I was dying and all he could do was sit there, staring at me as if I had simply mentioned something about going away for the weekend. And I *knew* he probably loved and needed me more than he loved and needed anyone else in this world. Probably more, even, than he did his mother. I wasn't about to let him get away with it, not this time. So I asked him, "Did you hear what I just told you?"

It took him a moment. He seemed paralyzed. Then he nodded.

"Do you understand what it means?" I asked.

He nodded again.

"Tell me," I said.

He wouldn't answer. Or he couldn't.

"*Tell* me," I insisted.

"You're very sick," he said. "You're going to die soon."

I nodded approvingly. A good answer. I might have been questioning him on some problems with his homework. "Are you sorry I'm going to die soon?" I asked.

He looked at me as though I had just slapped him again. His face was suddenly white. I was making progress. "Yes," he managed.

"So am I," I told him. "I wish I could have been able to hang around a little longer to watch you grow up. I know you're going to be quite a boy."

He didn't say anything.

"I love you very much," I said. "I want you to know that. I want you to remember it. I've always loved you. Maybe sometimes you didn't think I did. Maybe I didn't always seem to act that way. But that had nothing to do with you. That was just me. I've never felt anything but love for you. Do you understand that?"

He nodded.

"Good," I said. "Because that's important. It's also important for you to understand that it never made the slightest difference to me that you were my adopted son. I've never thought of you as anything but my son. Just, my son. I wish they'd never invented the word adopted. It's caused nothing but trouble. For everyone. If I had to do it over again, I'd never have even let anyone know you were adopted. Not even you. Then you wouldn't have had to worry so much about whether I really loved you. Do you think you'd have liked it better that way?"

He was just staring at the floor now, Norman. "Yes," he said.

"Sure," I said. "I knew it. But we had some pretty good times anyway, didn't we? Hey! Remember when you were just a little kid and we used to play cowboys in the living room?"

He looked up at me then but didn't answer.

"That was a pretty good game we had going there, wasn't it?" I said. "We used to shoot at each other from behind the furniture. Bang . . . bang! You're dead! But I was the one who always ended up getting shot. Remember?"

"Yes," he said.

"What happened then?" I asked. "I mean after I got shot?"

"I used to sing to you," he said. "A cowboy song. And you'd just lie there like you were dead."

"I remember that part," I said. "You were a good singer too. I mean, for such a little kid."

He was looking at me then, Norman, waiting for me to go on. But I wouldn't. I just sat there and didn't say anything. Finally, he had to pick it up himself.

"Don't you remember the end?" he asked.

"No," I lied.

"I used to kiss you and you'd come back," he said. "You wouldn't be dead anymore."

But he just barely got it out because he choked on the last of it as that beautiful peaches-and-cream face went all to pieces.

We hung onto each other.

My son has so much pain inside him, Norman. Only the smallest bit came out yesterday. When he's alone, he still sucks his thumb. He suffers because of it. I wish I could make him feel more secure, more loved before I leave him. There's not that much time, and I don't know how I'm going to do it. But I'm sure going to try.

November 1

I REMEMBER THE EXACT MOMENT, Norman, when my son first realized what it meant to be adopted. He had been hearing about being our "chosen child" and all the rest of it for years, but one summer day at the beach I happened to notice a small birthmark on his right arm and pointed out that I had a similar mark in almost the same place. It didn't surprise him. "Sure," he said. "That's because you're my daddy."

So with all our talk, all our indoctrination, he hadn't really grasped what being an adopted child meant. He had just been hearing a lot of words. So that day on the beach I compounded my original error by explaining it to him. At last it broke through.

He realized that not a single part of his mind or body came to him from the people he called Mommy and Daddy. And that night he wet his bed for the first time since he was toilet trained and didn't stop wetting it for almost three years.

But the ability to love isn't something that is passed on genetically. It's an acquired characteristic. Children can either reject it or accept it into the hospitality of their hearts. And I'm happy to say, Norman, that both my children chose to accept it. Judi and David can love. In their separate ways, they have learned how it's done. Which means, they *care*. Most of the credit for this goes to my wife. It was she who spent the most time with them during the important years. And she held back nothing. Because *she* knew how to love and care, *they* had the chance to learn to love and care.

Neither of our kids are "cool," Norman. Neither of them suffer from apathy, which is probably the worst, the most pathetic, the most far-reaching disease of our time. When all the trimmings are cut away, the most tragic human gesture of all is probably the shrug, that slight lifting of the shoulders that says, "What the hell. What difference does it make? Who cares?" That is the ultimate defense against the pain of loss. What you don't care about, what doesn't make any difference, can't hurt very much when you lose it. But then neither can it bring very much joy while you have it. Apathy is a total anesthetic. It eliminates all feeling, the good along with the bad. Finally, you end up being little more than an emotional zombie.

There are no emotional zombies in my family. We

all feel, we all care, we all love, we all hurt. My God,
do we hurt! It's been some days since I brought my
family into this, and we've been hurting like mad
ever since. There have been a lot of tears, a lot of
anguish. But I think most of that is over. I think it's
finally out of the way. And it helped. We all needed
the cleansing. *I* certainly did. I've had enough of trying to do it alone. If a man wants to, he can live
walled up within himself for a long time. But it's a
lot harder to die that way. However important love
may be to the process of living, it's doubly so to dying. By helping to support those I love, I find it much
easier to keep myself afloat. I can also give my kids
a little of what my grandfather gave me more than
thirty years ago, some feeling of continuity.

All right. So my son and daughter suddenly discover nature is tough: It's unyielding, it hits hard, it
takes away the people and things you hold dearest.
But it also offers guarantees of value: It gives love,
it hands out pleasures. There are all sorts of magic
landscapes to explore. My children are learning.
They're finding out life is great, life is endless. Until
it ends.

My family is even helping *me* discover things, Norman. I know they're doing some of it deliberately,
just to make me feel good. But I think most of it is
sincere and that this is how they really feel about it.
Not that the truth of it matters very much. What
matters is *why* they're doing it. And either way, the
motivation comes out love.

For one thing, my son has become more talkative,
more revealing than he has ever been at any time in

his life. He suddenly feels compelled to share every thought, every hope, every fragment of memory with me. He works hard at it. He tells me all the things he thinks I want most to hear. He tells me he wants to be a shrink just like me when he grows up. He tells me, actually *tells* me in so many words, Norman, how much he loves me. He says how proud of me he is, how he always brags to his teachers and the kids at school about how smart I am, how I take all these crazy nuts and turn them into regular people again.

He tells me things he remembers from all the way back when he was a very young child, a toddler— things he had never mentioned to me before. He recalls a rainy Sunday in the park when we were the only ones out feeding the ducks. He remembers when I once caught him by the collar to keep him from falling off a dock. He remembers the day I took the training wheels off his first two-wheeler and ran along with him, holding onto the bike until he was able to keep his balance. He remembers when he was once sick and I brought him home some toy soldiers with the heads broken off two of the red ones.

In fact he even remembers a fight I once had with some obnoxious, violently aggressive fool over a parking space. "You were really great," he tells me. "He was way bigger than you and you weren't even scared at all." He was wrong about that. I was so frightened my knees were shaking. But how could I back down in front of my seven-year-old son? The macho psychiatrist. The big brain. All that worldliness and sophistication, all that psychological knowledge and human understanding. And I still had to prove my manhood with my fists in a goddamned parking lot.

Yet my son remembered it. It was one of the things that had evidently impressed him most. How soft, how vulnerable, how subject to infection our children are, Norman. What marks we leave on them. What damage we can do. It's frightening, especially in retrospect. The wonder of it all is how well they somehow manage to turn out in spite of us.

My daughter is competing with my son in trying to fill me with love. It's easier for her. She has had more practice over the years. She does it well. She graces me with immortality. She tells me the same kind of stories my mother used to tell me when I was a skinny little kid who wouldn't eat his eggs. They make me seem better, finer, nobler than I am. They're made up of part memory, part sorrow, part truth, and part fiction. But mostly, they're made up of love. She's building me her own fortress out of it. She doesn't know anything about where I'm going, but she believes that wherever it happens to be, that what she's building will come in handy. And so do I. At one time during my daughter's growing up, she suffered from nightmares and was afraid of the dark. She was afraid that if she called for help, no one would come. I slept in her room for a few nights until the worst of it passed. I told her she didn't have to worry, that if she ever wanted or needed me I'd be there. She remembered and reminded me of that this morning. She told it to me innocently, lightly, pretending to be amused by the remembrance of such childish fears.

But she wasn't amused and she wasn't innocent of purpose. Her intentions were clear. She was showing me my old promissory note. And she wanted some assurance that when the due date arrived and she had to call it in, it would be honored.

I didn't know what I could do, but I did what I could for her. I told her things I didn't really believe, or that I half-believed, or wished I believed, or maybe even sometimes, when there suddenly seemed to be nothing else, that I *did* believe. I told her she'd never be alone as long as she loved, that, in one way or another, those she loved would always be with her and care about her and know she was there. I told her wherever she went with love inside her, she'd carry me there too.

But I felt uncomfortable telling her these things, Norman, almost embarrassed. It all seemed so childish, so pure, so sweet, so filled with hope. Yet what was my daughter if not a child—and pure and sweet and in desperate need of hope. So what else was I to say to her? That I was about to leave her forever, and that once I was gone, I'd be gone and that would be the end of me? That there was no such thing as the soul and that the only things she could be sure of in this world were getting hurt and saying goodby? And that when we did say goodby, all promissory notes were automatically cancelled and that it was tough luck but that was the way these things worked? Was *that* what I was supposed to say to her?

Hardly. I know better than that. But I can't help feeling embarrassed about what I *did* say to her. Even now, I can't be totally honest about it. Even now, when there's little left for me but the small satisfaction of being able to speak the absolute truth, I can't seem to get myself to be truthful about *this*. I still seem to be worried about sounding like some sort of crazy love fanatic, a kind of Holy Roller of the libido who believes the spirit of love is immortal, and that all those who love truly and well can count on being gifted with at least a reasonable facsimile of a soul. And if I—a medical man and a phychiatrist—were ever openly accused of such absurdly sentimental beliefs, I'd have to laugh and say, "Hey, you've got to be kidding!"

Except that I'm *not* laughing, Norman. And I'm *not* kidding. I'll say it now, because if I don't then everything in these tapes is a lie and I'm dying a fraud. I *do* believe what I told my daughter. I *do* believe that as long as she's capable of feeling love, she'll never be alone. I *do* believe that wherever she goes with love inside her, some small fragment, some small memory of me will go too. And I believe— although I may be embarrassed as hell at saying it aloud, at setting loose what I've kept hidden so quietly inside me for so long—I believe that if there is such a thing as a soul, then love is surely at its heart.

November 4

MY WIFE HAS BEEN SPENDING every possible minute
with me—both with the children and without them.
Frankly, Norman, I like it best when the two of us
are alone. I guess it was always that way. When
things were right for us, there was never anything
better. We were complete. In fact, I think the kids
sensed and resented it at times. We may have shut
them out, may have occasionally made them feel they
were in the way. And at certain times, I suppose they
were.

Last night we made love.

It has been years since the last time for us and it
was strange.

"*Can* you?" she asked.

"Am I dead yet?" I said.

She felt my pulse. "No," she told me.

"Then I can," I said.

And I could.

My God, how that woman knows me, Norman. But then I suppose I know her equally well. Which can be both good and bad. It was bad when we were living together at the end. It's been good this past week. Last night, it was superb.

"Tell me something nice," I said and held her.

"I love you," she said.

"And who's the greatest lover you've ever known?" I asked.

"You," she answered.

"Even now?"

"Even now," she told me.

"I guess you've gotten to be something of an authority on it these past years," I said and felt a wave of insane jealousy roll over me.

"Not really," she said. "What about you?"

"You spoiled them all for me," I told her. "I kept thinking of you. You wouldn't leave me alone."

"Good," she said. "Because you did the same to me. Twice, you actually stopped me from marrying."

This was how we stroked one another, Norman. What a love we felt. We carried it in our body juices. When we squeezed one another, it leaked like blood.

"Listen," I told her. "You can't go around being unmarried forever."

"I won't," she promised. But I was pleased to hear she didn't say it easily. What a rat I could be.

"What sort of a guy do you think you'll finally marry?" I asked.

"Oh, shut up," she said.

"No, really," I told her. "I think a first husband is entitled to some rights in this. He should at least know what to expect in the way of a successor."

"Stop it, you bastard," she said, not wanting me to go on with it. Yet I felt I had to, Norman. It was a very specific compulsion, an almost masochistic need to keep touching an open wound to make sure it still hurt. I was beginning to feel much too alive with her. I was floating too high. It worried me. I had to bring myself back down.

I said, "The kids will need a man around. I don't think you should let it drag too long without me."

"Oh, I won't," she promised. "How about the day after your funeral? Do you think that will be soon enough for the wedding? Or if you can give me a specific target date, we might even be able to arrange them both on the same day."

"Jesus Christ!" I said and startled her. "I just realized I haven't got a goddamned burial plot. All this time and I never once thought about it." Which wasn't true, Norman. I *had* thought about it, but just hadn't done anything about it.

She had turned her face away and wouldn't look at me. "If you don't stop that," she said, "I'm getting out of here this minute and I'm not coming back. And I mean it."

"I'm sorry," I told her and had a composite image of all the other times I had told her I was sorry over the years. I guess I had gotten to be pretty good at it. Maybe my son had trouble saying he was sorry, but I sure never did. At least, not with Barbara.

"Why do you have to do that to me?" she asked.

I had to let myself think about that one, Norman. I didn't want to give her any glib answers. "Because I'm frightened," I told her at last. "And because I love you. And because I need to feel loved in return. I've been alone with this for a long time. Now that you're here, I guess I'm taking advantage of it. I guess I have to see you hurting a little too."

"Don't you think I'm hurting without that?" she said.

"Yes," I told her. "But this is such a damned lonely thing. I had to make you show me."

She understood then and I was finally able to leave it alone. But I wasn't proud of myself and she knew me well enough to be aware of it. Lying beside me, she held my hand.

"Do you feel my hand?" she asked.

"Yes," I said.

"What else do you feel?" she asked.

"Love," I told her.

"Are you sure?" she said.

I nodded.

"And how long are you going to feel it?" she wanted to know.

"For as long as I can feel," I said.

"And after that?" she asked.

"I'll take it with me and still feel it," I said.

"Promise?" she said.

I nodded. But that wasn't enough. She wanted me to say it.

"*Promise?*" she said again.

"I promise," I told her.

I meant it, Norman. I do still. And I will.

****

ABOUT NORMAN GARBO

BORN AND RAISED IN NEW YORK, Norman Garbo is an artist who has also, over the past twenty years, lectured in most major cities as well as at universities throughout the United States. He has painted the portraits of three Presidents (Truman, Eisenhower, and Kennedy), had his work exhibited at the Metropolitan Museum, The Chicago Art Institute, and the Philadelphia Museum, and has written a syndicated column for the *Chicago Tribune*, New York News Syndicate, that appeared in a large number of newspapers in the United States, Canada, and England. Additionally, he has written many short stories for the *Saturday Evening Post* and other periodicals, as well as two best-selling novels, *Confrontation* (with Howard Goodkind) and *The Movement*. Mr. Garbo currently lives in Manhasset, Long Island.